# TOP GUN

# PROSPECTING

## FOR FINANCIAL PROFESSIONALS

# TOP GUN
# PROSPECTING

## FOR
## FINANCIAL
## PROFESSIONALS

### D. Scott Kimball

Dearborn™
Trade Publishing
A **Kaplan Professional** Company

Vice President and Publisher: Cynthia A. Zigmund
Acquisitions Editor: Mary B. Good
Senior Project Editor: Trey Thoelcke
Interior Design: Lucy Jenkins
Cover Design: Jody Billert
Typesetting: Elizabeth Pitts

© 2003 by D. Scott Kimball

Published by Dearborn Trade Publishing, a Kaplan Professional Company

Printed in the United States of America

03 04 05 10 9 8 7 6 5 4 3 2 1

**Library of Congress Cataloging-in-Publication Data**

Kimball, D. Scott.
    Top gun prospecting for financial professionals / D. Scott Kimball.
        p.   cm.
Includes index.
    ISBN 0-7931-7839-8
    1. Investment advisors—Marketing.  2. Success in business.   I. Title.
    HG4621.K495   2003
    332.6′068′8—dc21

                                                            2003014149

Dearborn Trade books are available at special quantity discounts to use
for sales promotions, employee premiums, or educational purposes.
Please contact our special sales department, to order or for more information, at trade@dearborn.com or 800-245-BOOK (2665), or write to Dearborn Financial Publishing, 30 South Wacker Drive, Suite 2500, Chicago,
IL 60606-7481.

Dedicated to those who have learned to love the hunt

# CONTENTS

Scott Kimball is not your typical financial advisor. You know this within a few minutes in his presence. He's been described as hard-nosed, confidently arrogant, talented, brilliant, cold, emotionless, energetic, passionate, an industry visionary. I don't know about any of that, but one of his clients said it this way: He can sell socks to snakes in summer. This guy is a good salesman.

I spent 20 years in the Navy, flew the now famous F-14 Tomcat, was a Top Gun graduate and instructor. In combat situations, your success or failure depends on your training and your ability to make split second critical decisions. You take responsibility for your success or failure because that success or failure is the direct result of the decisions you have made and the actions you chose to take. So it is in business on Wall Street. The techniques, strategies, and tactics you find in this book are the result of years of combat-tested military training and learning, as well as management techniques that have been used on the business battlefield for years to create, build, and defend the leadership positions of the world's greatest companies.

Scott has drawn from these best practices in creating the Top Gun Sales Program. I've known Scott for over 20 years and his passion for the salesperson is clear. As a managing director at a major Wall Street firm, he leads by example, elbow to elbow with his team, making cold calls next to people with only a few years in the business. At 40 years old, this guy gives you the sense that he's only getting started.

This book isn't written by a consultant who had a good year and retired from the daily grind. This is written by a street veteran who has built and rebuilt his own business and who has a clear passion for the service he provides, his clients, and his team. This book shares the insights of a career of nearly 20 years on Wall Street, from someone who never left the front lines of the business and is still there today. If you want to know what works—and what doesn't—then this is your prospecting bible.

Michael Patrick McGarvey
Management Consultant
San Diego, California

I would like to thank the many Top Gun financial advisors and professionals who were generous with their time and kind enough to share their experiences with me. It is from them that we truly learn the essence of what it takes to build a multimillion-dollar business in the financial service arena.

I would also like to thank Don Hull, the editor of my first published work. Don was the first publishing professional to recognize the potential of my ideas and writings and was a confidence-inspiring, intelligent source of energy for me.

To Richard Manchowicz, author and former Navy SEAL, for his help in clarifying the Top Gun Model. To Dr. Gail Davis Ph.D., author, professional performance coach, and psychologist, thank you for your guidance and clear thinking. Sue Knight, NLP expert and author of *NLP at Work,* thank you for your work and your gracious input.

I'd also like to thank someone who had the guts to join the U.S. Navy and fly around this and other countries, protecting our freedom: Michael Patrick McGarvey, a true Naval Aviator who flew the famous F-14 Tomcat out of Mirimar. Because of Mike and those like him, we can all rest a little easier each night.

To Bruce Faurot, a Top Gun advisor and personal confidant, you are one of the few in this business who brings a higher level of thinking to the game. Your clients are fortunate.

To my team, particularly Jason Adams, Brody Bray, and Tiffany McLaughlin, thank you for supporting me, driving me forward, and performing at a superior level every day.

I'd like to thank my wife Teri and children Connor, McCall, and Kelsey. There have been many entire days and nights in which I was sitting in front of a computer typing instead of at your side. As always, you have allowed me the freedom to do it. Someday, you'll see it was not in vain. No one has had more faith in me than Teri, who is herself a Top Gun in her profession.

I've been a fortunate man. There have been a lot of people who have taken a chance on me and given me an opportunity to perform. When that performance didn't materialize immediately, many of them kept the faith.

Finally, I'd like to say a special thank-you to my late mother-in-law, Aileen. When virtually all others had deserted me, she stood by my side and believed. In her own special way, she kept a wild Irish family together through all of the biggest challenges the good Lord could throw at a human being. Aileen was a fighter, a winner, and a leader. We should all be more like her.

What is Top Gun and why does it work? Top Gun attempts to utilize strategies and tactics that have been tested in the military, sports psychology, and business for decades and put them into a framework for you to apply to your business. The definition of a successful outcome of any military or competitive endeavor is to win—win the battle, win the war, win the game, win the medal, win the business, win the client. In various military strategies, from the ancient in Sun Tzu's *Art of War* to the modern tactics used in special operations teams like the Navy SEALs and the Advanced Fighter Weapons School (Top Gun), it is the *process* in which the actions are taken that leads to a win or a loss. The ability to define the mission, then, through planning, training, and consistent execution of strategies and tactics that are known to work, is how the mission is accomplished.

Today, landing the substantial financial client has become more competitive. Increasingly, and with success, teams have been formed at firms designed specifically to attack certain segments of the private client market. These teams are not unlike the special ops units of the military. They are usually small and highly skilled, move very quickly, are well trained, and are aggressive in their area of focus. They are on their game. They know how to get into the high-margin client. They go into a meeting knowing exactly what they want to accomplish. They know the landscape and the major issues and concerns that have to be addressed, and they know how to close. I'm sure you can agree that on many levels, there is a similarity to the highly skilled warriors in our military.

Top Gun is a means to an end. The means may not be perfect, and it may not appeal to everyone, but the end result accomplishes the critical mission of closing the performance gap in today's market environment. The model is built on a foundation that is firmly ethical and treats the client with respect. It is intuitively simple to understand and draws on basic business school instruction and military strategy that has been proven successful time after time, decade after decade, in war and in the battles we fight in the competitive arena we call everyday business.

Your mission is to build a practice, or build a better practice. Your mission is to become one of the elite in this industry, someone who is at the top of the business, who is one of the top 1 or 2 percent of the firm and top 10 percent in the business. You can't get there using hope as a strategy. You won't get there if you don't know what you're doing. You won't get there if you don't know what works and what doesn't. What works in this business at all levels, from beginner to managing director, is knowing how to find new business and bring it in. That process starts with prospecting. Prospecting is the name of the game. My mission is to help you get there, to give you the tools to accomplish your mission.

*Top Gun Prospecting* reveals the techniques used by top producers in the financial sales world for high-impact prospecting that will help in building the Top Gun book of clients—the 50 client relationships that will produce over $1 million in revenue for your business. If you are already producing above $1 million, using the strategies and tactics outlined here can take you to a new level of production. My objective is to have you look at your business differently than you ever have before. I can help you cut a clearer, cleaner path to enormous success. You'll focus in on your personal strengths and the strengths of your firm while minimizing your personal weaknesses and the weaknesses of your firm, whatever they may be. It's my goal to turn you into a highly motivated, highly efficient sales machine. And that begins with *prospecting*.

My mission here? To turn you into a *prospecting machine*. Good Luck.

# CHAPTER ONE

# THE FACTS OF LIFE

*The credit belongs to the person who is actually in the arena;*
*whose face is actually marred by dust and sweat and blood;*
*who strives valiantly; who errs and comes short again and again;*
*who knows great enthusiasm and great devotions;*
*whose life is spent in a worthy cause; who, at best, knows in*
*the end the triumph of high achievement and at worst,*
*if failure wins out, it at least wins with greatness,*
*so that this person's place shall never be with those*
*timid souls who know neither victory nor defeat.*

THEODORE ROOSEVELT

Sales consultants and so-called experts in the business give you their little diagrams and their lists of things to do and their formulas for success. This is fine, and I'm sure some of their stuff helps people, but it never helped me. I'm sure some of them actually were good salespeople at some point, but that may have been a long time ago.

I had to come up with this stuff on my own. Some of you helped me and I thank you for letting me have some of your time and expertise. Now I'm just sharing it with you. I'm not trying to make a living writing books or consulting with your firms. I have no dream of starting my own firm. I work for a living at a Wall Street firm. I make my cold calls, meet with new people and come in every day, just like you, and am expected to make something happen. I have to overcome the same issues you do each day, maybe more. I am you. This is a book written by someone in the trenches with you every day *right now*. Everyone wants to make things so complex. Top Gun is simple. There's no excuse for not using it if you think it can help you.

Let me speak frankly. If you currently work at a major firm in the capacity of advisor, broker, or consultant in the financial services business, and you do not have a business model that will have you producing over $1 million annually within the next 2 or 3 years, I'm here to tell you that *your days are numbered.* You can either figure out what you're going to do in another line of business or you can figure out how to get to the magic number—and soon. If you don't, you will not get the resources, you will not get the attention, and you will not get the support of your firm going forward.

Here's the deal: Wall Street firms have changed their perspective rather dramatically of late. In an extended bull market, they tried to be everything to everyone, promoting the "one-stop shop" concept. In an extended bull market, that can work, I suppose. When the pendulum swung in a different direction, they realized that without focus, without cost controls and proper allocation of resources, they were losing money, and lots of it. Now we're in what could be an extended bear market, or at least I think it's fair to say, a more normalized market, that may not produce the kinds of returns to investors we have seen in the recent past. It's possible that we may not see another bull market for ten or fifteen more years. Are you prepared for that? Is your firm? You can bet your firm is taking the necessary steps to deal with the new environment and make sure they can ride it out. What have you done?

Today the focus is on profitability and market *niche*. The firms want everyone to focus on the profitable client, the high net worth client. A few years ago they were handing out awards and trips to people if they opened 500 IRA accounts, despite the fact that none of those accounts were profitable, and punishing those who opened up ten or fifteen accounts totaling $30 or $40 million. Of course, the fact that these accounts were actually profitable to the firm was irrelevant. The geniuses have even decided to change what they call us once again: *Wealth Managers.*

Over time, our job description has been customer's man, broker, account executive, financial consultant, financial advisor, and now, wealth manager. This nice-sounding title is misused in nearly every case in the industry, and designed to appeal to people with over $1 million in investment assets. Don't get messed up with the titles, just understand that this is simply marketing. Know that your business is still the same— providing people (or institutions) with returns on their investments based on the highest level of thinking, along with the best advice and service you and your firm can deliver. That has not and will not ever change.

The big firms have focused on this higher end of the market for an obvious reason. It's profitable, at least *more* profitable than the smaller accounts, because the client with over $1 million can use the substantial expertise and specialized products and services of the firm. If you've never been on the trading floors of one of the bigger firms, I'll tell you this: The people in those rooms have more knowledge of the markets and how not only to create, but to financially engineer almost anything you can dream of, than any one place on earth. This is why New York is the financial capital of the world. These people are the brainpower that runs the world's money machine. These firms employ some of the smartest people I have ever met in New York. These people make *billion* dollar decisions in a day. I call this *firepower.* The smaller account wants to trade at three cents, with no account fees and free online trading and free online account access. They want free financial plans and free advice. This is fine. If this appeals to you, you can get it online at "www.do-it-yourself-free-you-get-what-you-pay-for-financial-plans.com." But the firms providing this type of service to clients don't need a whole lot of brainpower and capital to serve this client. The client at this level is not making use of the firepower of the firm and, therefore, is not a high-margin client to the firm.

This fact of the marketplace is causing Wall Street firms with well-paid, well-trained financial sales forces with plenty of firepower behind them to adapt. To maximize their utility and profitability, they've had to make a choice to either move upstream or downstream. That is, to find clients who utilize the firms' expertise, capital, and financial engineering (the firepower), or to get rid of all those people, buy a few more computers, put all their clients online to fend for themselves and provide little, if any, human contact or financial advice. The big players have picked their direction and the market has been segmented. Major firms have gone upstream, seeking the higher net worth accounts that can make use of the expertise and financial engineering capabilities of the firm. Others have staked out ground in the discount brokerage business or the online trading business. A couple of firms are still stuck in the middle, doing a little of both—not fully committed in either direction. If they want to survive, a commitment one way or the other will have to be forthcoming. They'll get there.

If you don't get anything else from this book, get this: Prospecting is not purely a mathematical endeavor. It is not "just a numbers game" as you've been told over and over again by the "experts." If it were, then computers that dial 500 numbers a day with a recorded sales message would have the same ratio of success as a human being. But they don't. Prospecting in our business, like sales in general, involves human contact 99 percent of the time, and therefore, is an event in which the nuances and psychology of human interaction can and do have an enormous impact. This is why someone who is "a good prospector" has a success ratio dramatically higher than someone who is not. It also explains why one person can make 50 contacts in a day and make appointments with five or ten people, and the person next door can make 50 contacts using the same list and make one appointment. In this book, and in my life, I have proven it. The human element is crucial. Don't ever let anyone tell you otherwise. Successful prospecting is much more than numbers.

In my first book, *Top Gun Financial Sales*, I spoke of a different way of doing business. In essence, I talked about working smarter rather than working harder. I suggested a model that involved fewer clients and better service. For some people, the idea was absurd—at first. More clients automatically equaled more money, right? Those of you with some economics or business school in your background may recall the concept of the law of diminishing returns. The idea is that simply producing more of something doesn't mean that the rate of return on it stays constant. More of something often can bring a business to its knees. At the extreme, once something has reached a level of production beyond its optimal level, you begin to see diminished, and then negative, rates of return. This question came up in thinking about our business: At what point does adding another small account to our practice begin to erode our effectiveness, our efficiency, our ability to do high-margin business with high-margin clients? So finding that optimal level of client relationships became the quest.

If you look at most of the truly large producers, the Top Gun business model isn't substantially different than what they've been doing for years. It just didn't have a name before. Most of these people have 50 (or fewer) great clients with whom they do business. They focus on providing something for their clients that drives down the heart of their strengths, as well as the strengths of their firms. They put the clients' needs first, above their own. They are honest and forthright and can be trusted to give the best advice possible. They deliver on their promises, no matter how small, and they never overpromise. They communicate. Big producers don't have time to waste dealing with dead-end clients, so they simply don't get involved with them from the get-go. On the other hand, they give freely of themselves to their sacred 50. Top Gun producers do high-margin, low-risk business. They make heroes of their clients. And most important, they understand the power of the relationship.

I realize there are still people out there who truly believe that *any* client is a good client. Personally, I believe only a *good* client is a good client. To me, a good client is one for whom hard work is a pleasure. But others are so fear-driven they don't dare turn down any kind of business—even the kind of business that takes up their time, energy, and patience without any real return on their investment. They're afraid of their managers, afraid of their clients, and afraid of trying something new or taking any kind of risk at all. These people cannot wrap their heads around the idea that you can have a better quality of life by working for fewer clients, dropping clients, and adding the right kind of client, and only a few of them. To them, this seems too dangerous, too radical, too outrageous. Unless their firm tells them to do it, they wouldn't think of it. Well, I'm here to tell you that your firm is looking at this very hard. Some have already begun to tell their people to start thinking about how to be more efficient and more profitable. One even sent an e-mail around with a Top Gun excerpt attached and told his troops, "This is how business needs to be done around here from now on." It reminds me of a quote:

> *All truth passes through three stages.*
> *First, it is ridiculed.*
> *Second, it is violently opposed.*
> *Third, it is accepted as being self-evident.*
> ARTHUR SCHOPENHAUER (1788-1860)

One of the Top Gun advisors I work with produced over $4 million in 2002 and he has fewer than ten clients. Frankly, this is too focused and exposes him to greater risk, but he works hard, knows his stuff, and has focused his business in one area in which the firm has a very strong competitive advantage. He's doing everything outlined in *Top Gun Financial Sales*. He gets it. Spending more time on clients and firms that appreciate his expertise and are engaged in the relationship has paid off for him in a far bigger way than trying to please everyone in every way.

I get e-mails and letters every day from financial advisors and financial salespeople at all levels of the business, from large and small investment and insurance firms all over the country. The Top Gun model has struck a cord and is having an impact on people's lives all over the country. Seasoned producers have read the book and are appreciative that someone has bothered to tell it like it is. Producers looking for a model to take them to the next level tell me they now have a clear path, that Top Gun helped them define their business and the direction they'll be going. Struggling producers have found the inspiration to go on and keep at it despite difficult times.

Don't be confused. Reading a book isn't going to change your business. Taking *action* is what changes things in your life. One of my favorite things to say is that your success or failure will be the result of the sum total of the decisions you make and the actions you take or fail to take. Where you are today is the cumulative result of the decisions you have made up to this moment. Read that again. Go back and read that sentence again and think about it. Okay, I'll write it again. *Where you are today is the cumulative result of the decisions you have made up to this moment.* You know what this means, don't you? You have to take responsibility for where you are because you are there because of the decisions *you* made. Surprisingly, this is too tough for most people.

You're not a failure because your daddy didn't give you enough lovin', or your mommy was an alcoholic. You're where you are because you made choices that led you here. If *here* is a good place, full of success and happiness, then good for you. You've made some fine choices and you should be proud of yourself. If *here* isn't so great, if you're failing at the moment, know that it isn't too late to turn the boat around. All you have to do is choose to take different actions. Choose not to be average. Choose to move *through* your fears. Break on through to the other side. Chart a new course.

Why should you make these choices? Because, whether you like it or not, you will own your success or failure in the end, no matter how hard you try to blame others. That's the truth, and we both know it.

> *The difference between a successful person and others*
> *is not a lack of strength, not a lack of knowledge,*
> *but rather a lack of will.*
> VINCE LOMBARDI

> *When you have to make a choice and don't make it,*
> *that in itself is a choice.*
> WILLIAM JAMES

Look at Figure 1.1. The three circles are the areas of your work life that you deal in every day. In the center are things you can control. Around that, in the second circle, are things you can influence but that you don't control. In the outermost circle are things in which you have an interest, but for which you have no influence or control.

The circles in the diagram can expand or contract depending on your actions and your performance. Interestingly, if you do very well in executing on the things over which you have control, your circle of influence will expand because you will be brought in to influence other situations, and perhaps end up controlling them, which will expand your control center. This is how the world works. The objective is to expand your center of control.

**FIGURE 1.1    Circles of Control**

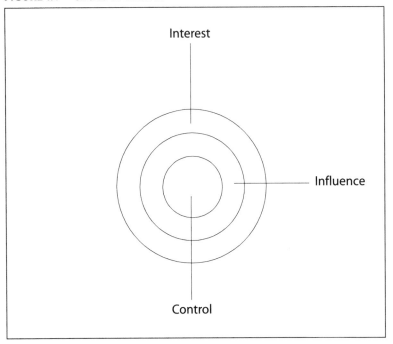

The reality is that most people spend most of their time and energy in the outer circle, the only place where they have no control or influence, worrying about, complaining about, or trying to control or influence things over which they have no control. In other words, they try to work from the outside in. The net result is that the more time you spend doing this, the more your center of control diminishes in size. This is not good. This is not the objective. This leads to failure.

In our business of financial sales, there are a lot of things we cannot control. I would contend that the two most important things we can control are our own actions and our attitude. When you are going about your day, the actions you take, or fail to take, will be the mark of your success or failure that day. As each day piles up one atop another, the cumulative effect of your daily actions will add up to your success or failure in the business. This fact led to one of the most important Top Gun rules of engagement mentioned in my first book: Do your push-ups every day. For the Top Gun producer, this means making at least the minimum number of outbound calls or face-to-face appointments with new people *every day.*

So when you look at your business, you need to look at your actions first. Are you spending too much time thinking about, working on, or worrying about things over which you have no control or influence? Are you worried about where the market is headed or whether your boss likes you best? These are things over which you have no control.

What would happen if instead you worried about and devoted productive time and energy to devising portfolios or finding financial solutions to your existing clients, in order to ensure that they were in good shape despite market conditions? What if you focused your time and efforts on prospecting for better clients in order to grow your business and revenue so that you become one of the top producers in the office, if not the firm? I'll tell you what will happen. Your boss probably *will* like you best! Focusing on taking action and becoming successful in the areas over which you do have control will lead to your success. Do the opposite and you undermine yourself and greatly reduce your prospects for success.

One of the most important things over which we do have control is our effort to prospect for new business. Prospecting is at the core of our ability to succeed in our business. I remember once talking to a sales manager at a large investment firm about the people he likes to hire, and he told me that he prefers someone who isn't from a rich family. He prefers someone who is smart, hungry, and has no contacts. This surprised me, so I asked him why. He said that in his experience, whenever he'd hired people based on their wealthy contacts, it didn't work out the way he expected. He found that they'd start off making 50 to 100 phone calls to the people they knew, or to their rich family members, and even if they had some degree of success, that success never seemed to last. Once they'd blown through everyone they knew, they came to a standstill. They didn't have the right stuff to pick up the phone, call people they didn't know, and ask for an appointment to talk about one of the most personal matters—their money. Few people have the right stuff to do that, which is why few people make it in this business. It's also why most people don't last in this business for five years before they quit or wash out. The old saying goes, if it was easy and everyone could do it, everyone would.

Results are the only thing that matters—results for your clients, for your firm, and for you. If your clients aren't getting the results, they'll leave you. If your firm isn't getting results from you, you'll be the one leaving. If you aren't getting results, you won't get paid, because, as you know, this isn't, as a rule, a salary plus bonus job. There are no excuses in our business, just reasons for not performing. In our positions, we cannot allow ourselves to buy into the mind-set of making excuses. Once you've done that, all hope is lost. The market is lousy, my boss hates me, the firm is screwed up, my clients won't listen to me, and on and on. The fact is that someone in your firm is right now having a record year. He or she is blowing the doors off and doing millions in fees or commissions, and you're not. It's that simple. This is your wake-up call to get in the game and be one of those professionals having the record year instead of one of those making excuses. It starts with your frame of mind, your resolve to be one of the best, taking a hard look at your business and how you should reorganize your priorities, thinking about the actions you take during a day, or fail to take each day, that are undermining your ability to succeed or move forward. It starts with getting on the phone and talking to people. It starts with getting out and meeting people. And it starts with you and the actions you take or fail to take. Doing nothing, hoping for things to change, is a conscious decision also, just as it is to do something. Be the catalyst for change in your life and in your career. Don't wait for someone or something else to do it.

The sales process is divided into three distinct parts: prospecting, selling, and closing. Prospecting is the first and most critical element of your future success. It, too, is a process comprised of three essential elements: name gathering, filtering, and appointment setting. You gather names, you filter them down to the qualified leads, and then you set appointments to meet them so you can begin selling. You cannot take prospecting for granted. You can't even look at it as a necessary evil. If you want to be Top Gun, you have to *love it* because it's a challenge. Finding a qualified prospect is great, but getting through to the person you need to speak with and actually booking an hour or so is very difficult. Sales is an *art*. The design of the presentation, the nuance of reading body language, the fluctuation of tone and placement of emphasis, and the timing and style of the close are at least 50 percent an artistic endeavor.

It has been said that prospecting is purely a *mathematical* endeavor, that there is very little artistry about it. I disagree. Even though the most creative prospecting campaigns ultimately come down to an algorithm or equation, you'll never get to that equation without artistry. The success in prospecting isn't simply about the number of calls you make. It has to do with the proper selection of whom to call, when to call, what to say, and how to say it. After that, successful prospecting comes from the process, the consistency of your daily actions. If you are consistent in the way you go about finding the right kinds of prospects, consistent in how you approach them, consistent in your message to them, consistent and clear in your message and your execution of a valid investment strategy, then your numbers will be there. You'll be a prospecting machine.

To do this, you need to know what works and what doesn't. That begins with knowing whom you're going after and why. It's important to align your prospecting efforts with your desired results. There is no point in wasting time going after clients who can't bring you the kind of business you say you're looking for. For example, you've probably heard someone say that they have a goal of landing at least one huge gorilla client each year. But do they call on these people? No. So how will they land one?

Using a baseball analogy, let's look at Barry Bonds, one of the great homerun hitters of our day. Each pitch is a prospect for his next home run. Does Barry swing at every pitch? No. He selects that pitch that he knows he has the highest probability of hitting out of the park. He doesn't always hit it, and when he does, it isn't always a homerun, but the selectivity of his swings is part of the equation of his success. He intelligently and patiently selects the pitches that he can most often hit out of the park. If it isn't one of those pitches, he won't swing at it unless absolutely necessary. So it is in your business. You only have so many hours in the day, so many calls you can make, so many people you can e-mail. If you're doing it right, you can build a vast and successful business. If you do it wrong, you will feel like you're working hard for nothing. You'll be left feeling frustrated and confused as to why you failed.

If this is the way you feel now, it's probably time to rethink the way you're doing your business. There is business to be had out there for all of us. Your frustrations aren't due to a bad market. It doesn't matter whether we're in a recession or in an expansion, inflationary times or deflationary times. There are no excuses. You have to own your results, good or bad, despite market conditions.

Look around you. People in the business are kicking ass, even in the worst economies! You're fooling yourself if you try to blame your failures on something remote like the market, your wife, your husband, your kids or parents, the weather, your manager who has it in for you, your firm, or *anything* other than the way you do your business. Want to spot a loser? Listen to them talk about how tough the market is and how any failure to do business is due to something other than him- or herself. When Barry Bonds strikes out, he doesn't blame his team.

A homerun hitter in baseball comes up to bat in the right frame of mind. He isn't going up to the plate thinking he will strike out. You can't go into a prospecting call or sales presentation thinking you're going to fail. Go in confident that this prospect will become a client today, that on this call you will find that "holy grail" client. Go into the call or meeting knowing you are prepared, that you are the best in the business, and that this prospect may not know it yet, but he or she needs you. Go up to the plate mentally prepared to hit a homerun. As you hit more homeruns, they get easier to hit. Your confidence builds, you start swinging with more authority and confidence. You win because you believe you are a winner, and people can feel that. People love to work with winners. Here, in America, we do not like losers. We don't want to be around losers; we don't want to be associated with losers. Remember the Christopher Lasch quote: "Nothing Succeeds like the appearance of success."

An interesting thing I've found about top producers is that *they read books like this one.* They read every book on the business that comes out! Why? Because even if they only get one good idea out of it, it's worth the money. Even if they are simply reminded of what they already know, but the book helps them refocus or redefine their business for the next 6 to 12 months, it was worth the money.

The bottom line is this: If you cannot prospect effectively and efficiently, you will fail in this business. My mentor in this business told me when he hired me that he was going to teach me everything he knew about the business. This was exciting, right up until he told me that we would start by gathering names. He showed me that the process of a sale started with deciding whom we wanted as clients. Then we gathered up all those names and refined them, filtered through them, and ended up with a group we could call to try and meet with face to face. This seemed mundane to me at first, but after years of practice, I became quite proficient and this skill has served me well.

Now, whenever I read magazines or newspapers, I'm subconsciously looking for the names of people that fit the profile I want as clients. When I eat at a restaurant, my eye seeks out the top three people who appear to be the type with whom I'd like to do business. My best clients are people who came out of newspapers or directories, people I reached out to in some way, not the other way around, not referrals, not direct mail, not seminars, not family members. I know that it is politically correct to tell everyone that your business is all from referral, but I think that most people in our business who say that are lying. It's a bunch of bull. I know, because I've talked to hundreds of people in this business privately and asked them to tell me the truth, and they will admit it. So prospecting is important, so important that I was asked to write this book. I didn't have to sell the idea to a publisher, they asked me, because their clients, who are brokerage firms, banks, insurance companies, asked them for it. If everyone has so many referral clients, why is everyone asking for a book on how to do it the way I've done it for 20 years? Because that's the way it's done, that's why.

So don't feel like an outcast at the next meeting when someone asks the crowd where they get most of their clients, and someone prods them to say "Referrals mostly, right?" It's bull for most advisors.

Many financial consultants *have* built their businesses on seminars, radio shows, advertising, and/or referrals. We'll go into all the ways to find clients. What works for me may not work for you, and vice versa. It will be interesting to see a variety of ways that the Top Guns get new business. There's no one right place to find a new client. There are many pathways to success. You may find a few new ideas about your own path right here in this book.

Great salespeople are not necessarily naturals; it's very often a learned trait. I've worked with some of the smartest people on Wall Street, and they can't sell. I've worked with people from some of the wealthiest families in the country, and they can't sell. Your family connections and the number of letters you have after your name won't necessarily make you a good salesperson. But, I've worked with people who have an IQ just a notch above a golden retriever, and they do very well. Why? If it's not brains, family ties, or academic degrees, it must be something else. What is the essence of being a great salesperson? The greatest successes in sales are those people who have a relentless desire to succeed, make things happen, and connect with people on a personal level. In our business, that starts with being a highly efficient prospecting machine.

Prospecting for clients never changes. Sure, market conditions change. Bull markets and bear markets call for a potentially different approach, but the process of prospecting for new clients never changes. As I point out in *Top Gun Financial Sales*, the Top Gun producer never, ever, ever stops prospecting. Your lead or your pitch may change, the product or service focus may change, but you still have to gather names of potential clients from somewhere, filter through those names, and convert them into clients in some reasonable period of time. Successful salespeople have learned how to do this efficiently. If you haven't, I'm hoping I can help. If you have, I'd like to turn up the volume a bit and teach you how to increase the ratio of your conversions (changing a prospect into a client).

I've been told that a lot of people in our business stopped prospecting during the last bull market. If that's true in your case, you may be a bit rusty. Your wheels may just need a little grease, but then you'll be off and running again. Of course, if you started your career during this last bull market, it's possible you were never really tested in the true sense of the word.

The true test of a great financial consultant is how he or she performs in a bear market. This is when it's tough, right? This is when nobody wants to talk to you and nobody seems to have any money to invest.

Bull! *This is the best time to prospect.* It just feels tough. If you don't use this opportunity to prospect like a mad man or woman, you're missing out of one of the biggest opportunities you will ever see in your career. Trust me, these kinds of opportunities don't come along but two or three times in a person's career. This is when you pick up market share. Think about it. Everyone is moaning about the market and the lack of business. Nobody is calling anyone. Everyone is just hoping that they can get through the day without getting fired and make a little money. This is when you can go out and gather up all the good clients in the country. This is when people are starved for advice and guidance. This is when the older brokers are throwing in the towel and the younger ones can't believe how their world has changed, that this business is "just too tough." This is when people quit. You can grab the golden clients who wouldn't have thought of moving their accounts a few years ago. Now, everything is up for grabs. It's open season. Nobody is off limits. You just have to go and get them. If you act now, you can come out on the other side of a tough market positioned to make more money than you ever dreamed.

Nobody wakes one day just knowing how to prospect. It's something you learn. The greatest prospectors have the right mind-set, keep their eyes on the prize, don't take rejection personally, are organized, have a process in place, are focused on a niche, and are creative and real in their approach.

Prospecting is an essential tool, central to a financial advisor's or consultant's ability to build or rebuild a client "book" and become successful in this business. There are many techniques and many ways to prospect, many of which I'll discuss here. As I've said before, not every style of prospecting fits every type of personality. It's important to find what works for you. I'll share the ones I feel will get you to the top faster than others, but ultimately the choice is yours. It's like exercise, the kind that works is the kind you *do.*

When I first entered this business, my mentor told me, "I'm going to teach you how to be the best prospecting machine in America. If I can do that, then they can drop you out of a helicopter into the middle of any English-speaking city in the world and you'll be able to build a business with just yourself, a phone, and a phone book." He was right.

After building a book in California, I moved across the country to Atlanta. I knew one person in Atlanta, and he gave me a room to stay in for four weeks. He didn't have money or contacts that would help me. So, from a business standpoint, I was starting from ground zero. But because I had the skills and the right mental frame of mind to prospect effectively, I was able to build a productive book from scratch by picking up the phone, talking to people. As soon as I got in front of them, I started opening accounts.

This book will teach you how to become a highly effective prospecting machine. It will get you in the right frame of mind, and tell you true prospecting stories that you can take with you every day as you encounter resistance and need inspiration.

# CHAPTER TWO

# THE FUNDAMENTALS— TOP GUN FOR FINANCIAL PROFESSIONALS

*It is not our preferences that cause the problem*
*but our attachment to them.*

BUDDHA

Let's look at this quote and use it as a basis for an exercise to further gain your commitment to Top Gun. First, answer some questions to get to the truth:

1. Is it possible that simply continuing to do what you've been doing will result in a different outcome in the near future?

2. Is it possible that every one of your clients is currently content and happy with their performance over the past year and the level of service you are providing?

3. Is it physically possible for one person to properly service the needs of 1,000 or 2,000 accounts?

4. Is it physically possible for one person to talk to 1,000 relationships in one day? One week?

5. Is it possible for one person to give serious thought and analysis to 100 or more individual accounts on a timely basis?

Five questions. The answer to each is likely no. Common human nature is to solve this dilemma with harder work. Working harder will make things better, so we think. This is wrong. It is an exercise in futility to simply continue to work harder, do the same thing over and over again with more frequency expecting the outcome to be different. It is impossible for all your clients to be content and happy with the level of service you're providing if you haven't spoken to most of them in the past three to six months. What's the point? What an empty feeling, looking at an account page and not knowing who those people are. It's an empty feeling for them as well, I suspect.

During the weeks following the September 11th attacks in our country, I had my hands full simply taking care of the 50 relationships I handled. I cannot imagine what it must have been like for someone who has 500 relationships. No, you cannot physically handle the demands of that many accounts, you cannot *really* talk to that many relationships in one day or one month, and you cannot give serious thought to their accounts.

The fact that people can't provide their best clients with their best thinking or the time and effort those clients deserve is at the heart of the problems that face our industry right now.

Clients aren't happy, financial consultants aren't happy, and firms aren't happy. Clients' account performance is less than satisfactory, consultant production is terrible, and the firm is trying to figure out how to deal with the fact that they have a huge profitability problem with a very large number of their producers.

I call these issues the *performance gap.* There is a performance gap between the expectations of the clients and actual results. There is a performance gap between the level of production of the average financial advisor, broker, or consultant and the cost of maintaining a seat. There is a performance gap in the amount of expertise and knowledge required to do an excellent job in this business and the level of expertise that exists. Top Gun is designed to close the performance gap.

In *Top Gun Financial Sales: How to Double or Triple Your Results While Reducing Your Book,* the first book in the Top Gun series, I outlined such things as the principles of the Top Gun business model, the keys to success, the nine reasons for failure, the concept of Margin, Probability, and Risk, as well as how to use SWOT, the Boston Matrix, and the CARVER Matrix to determine *what* business to go after and why. These are important to know in order to fully understand the reasoning behind Top Gun prospecting.

First, the Top Gun Business Model is designed for the existing financial consultant, advisor, or salesperson to increase business—but not by 10 or 20 percent. It is designed to increase production 100 percent or more. A new hire should take the time to read *Top Gun* if only to know how to move ahead in the business with a plan for success and to avoid the pitfalls that so many of us have experienced along the way. Specifically, the model has produced actual results—a $2 million producer has seen business increase to $6 million, a $350,000 producer has seen business increase to $1.2 million, a $750,000 producer has become a $2 million producer.

These results were not achieved in the middle of a bull market or at the top of the bubble in the tech sector. These results were achieved in a decline of the economic cycle, and during a crash in the tech sector, and in the following market malaise in which Wall Street laid off more than 65,000 people. The model works. It works in good times and in bad times. It works for professionals with historical production in the millions and for those with $200,000 in annual business. It works if you're 25 years old or you're 55 years old.

With the Top Gun Business Model, there are no excuses for failure. You can't blame your results on your branch manager, the market, lousy parents, or lack of education. You win or you lose on your own merits. You accept your results and you own them. You can take credit for your success fully and responsibility for your failures fully. Top Gun advisors fail in many ways every day. But they don't fail to achieve their ultimate objective, which is to be in the top 10 percent of producers nationwide.

I've stated many times that the new base number on Wall Street will very shortly be $1 million. If you don't want to get there, then put this book down right now. Let someone else read it, someone with the desire and hunger to stay in this business.

The thinking behind *Top Gun for Financial Professionals* was really drawn from many places—the Navy's Advanced Fighter Weapons Training School, the Navy SEALs, and Wharton Business School, as well as noted management consulting firms like Boston Consulting. Some of the techniques come from studies that serious behavioral psychologists and economists have done over the years that tell us a lot about people. All of it adds up to a way of looking at yourself, your business, and your clients differently from this point forward. If you adopt it, you will find yourself working on a whole new level of efficiency, productivity, and profitability, and you can make more money than you've ever made in your life in this business, good times or bad.

## The Underlying Belief System

There are only three underlying central beliefs in Top Gun. First, that you make a decision not to be average. Second, change is something to be embraced. And third, responsibility for your success of failure lies only with you and the decisions you make every day. You, and you alone, will own the cumulative results of those decisions in the end.

### Decide Not to Be Average

Someone once said, "You are today at the very place in your life that is the sum total of all your decisions up to this point in time." That's powerful. Think about it. We all make thousands of decisions every day. We decide when to get out of bed, take a shower, brush our teeth, go to work, smile at our assistant, pick up the phone to call someone, be enthusiastic, drive safely on the way home, pick up some flowers or a gift for the spouse, greet the kids enthusiastically, take a walk, work out, read to the kids or help them with homework, go to a child's basketball game, rock the baby to sleep, and/or to talk with the spouse in a moment of quiet.

At any point in that day you could decide not to go to work, to frown at your assistant, to go in your office or not talk to anyone on the phone. You could skip your child's basketball game and go to a bar and drink and/or ignore your spouse. Every decision has a consequence, a result. Perhaps not immediate, but there is a sort of cumulative effect our decisions create of which we're often unaware because it happens slowly.

You have the power to decide that you will not settle for being average. You will strive to be the best, or the best you can be, which is no doubt far above average. You can decide that change is good, and to embrace it openly with a positive outlook. Companies make decisions every day that may not appear to make sense to us. You have to try to see the opportunity in it for you and for your team and your clients. If a series of decisions is being made that endangers your way of life or job or your clients' financial interests, you have the power to make a change yourself. You can make a decision and make a change. You can decide to stick it out and work through it. Either way, the results are yours. You own it. If things don't work out the way you had planned, you can't go around blaming the company. It was your decision to stay there.

You can choose to recognize that the place you ultimately end up, how you end up spending your life, will be the direct result of the decisions you make along the way. Sometimes when I hear people talking about their lives when they're older, I can tell immediately what kind of person they were when they were younger. I can tell when people spent their lives drifting in the wind and just sort of letting things evolve. There they are, in retirement, sitting there talking to you on their porch in Florida, and they can't really even tell you how they ended up there. It just sort of happened. It wasn't because they made a decision to end up there.

The decision not to be average lies in the ability to execute consistently day in and day out. This is the difficult part of being Top Gun. It's easy to occasionally work hard or efficiently, its quite another thing to do it day in and day out. Let me give you an example of the power of consistency.

I recently visited a couple in their 90s. He never made more than $22,000 per year. They put four children through college and live humbly in the same home they built with their own hands and where they raised their children. They owe nothing to anyone. They live simply and modestly and don't care about fancy clothes or cars. They're not concerned with what they don't have. They care about their family, about having their loved ones know that they're loved. They care about their friends and their neighbors. They care about church and God.

The wife has been going around the house and picking up the loose change her husband leaves on countertops and dresser tops for around 40 years. Every week she deposits the loose change into one account, a passbook savings account at the local bank. She pulled out the passbook and showed it to me. There is $31,000 in that account. Remember that this is just the loose change rolling around the house that most people overlook! I exclaimed, "WOW," and she said, "You think that loose change rolling around your house doesn't mean much or that it won't amount to anything? Better take a second look, sonny!" This is the power of the cumulative effect of a decision to do something consistently over time. It was her choice to be consistent about picking up that money and depositing it in a special account.

The first time you come home drunk after work, it may not immediately ruin your relationship, but perhaps after the 100th time your spouse will walk out. This is a dramatic example, but it applies. If you come in every day and fall into a routine of not picking up the phone, you may not see your business suffer the first day, or even the first year, but eventually, your business will die. I call this the cumulative effect of nonaction.

There is a school of thought that believes that you don't have any control over how things go in your life, that fate controls all, and we're just sort of here to accept whatever fate has in store for us. These people are called fatalists. There are many things we can't control and it's important to recognize those things and let go of them. Equally important is recognizing what we *can* control and acting upon those things. We can surely control our actions and our attitude. We can control how we treat people each day. We can control how many times we pick up the phone to make a new contact. We can control our decision to go to that networking meeting, give that seminar, or make that extra effort to stop by and see someone on the way home from work. It is these things we can control that will make all the difference in the end. They are subtle, it takes time for the cumulative effect of these decisions to add up to success, but they will add up and the results will be there.

Recently a financial consultant in our community died. I didn't know him, but many people did. I was told that at his funeral there were so many people in attendance that they flowed outside the church and into the street at the largest church in Atlanta. People who thought they knew him well were amazed to find during the eulogy that he had done many amazing things, not the least of which was give his time, energy, and money to numerous charitable causes. He visited friends and clients and people who were friends of friends at the hospital when they weren't well. He quietly paid the water, light, and heating bills for people he knew who couldn't afford to do it themselves. He gave more than he took. He did it consistently, and look at that crowd, the result of consistent right action on the part of one man.

## Embrace Change

Change is constant, as they say. Our business has seen huge changes in the past ten years. More will come I'm sure. If we can't get our heads around that fact, if we are always thinking about the way things used to be and how much better it was in the good old days, we're dead. It's over. You have to look at change as opportunity. This can be hard when that change is moving you from something you're comfortable with to something you don't know. Change can seem hard if you let it. Instead, if you look at it as a part of life, and learn to roll with it and take advantage of it, finding ways to make it work to your benefit, then change is suddenly *your* friend while it is the enemy of the man next to you.

Change is imminent. If you embrace it, it will enhance your life. If you don't, it could ruin you.

## Accept Responsibility for Both Success and Failure

In your life, have you ever blamed something that happened to you on someone else? You know, thought to yourself, *he did that to me* or *if it wasn't for her, I wouldn't be in this position.* We've all done it. But we know, if we think about it, it's not the truth. Usually, we let it happen to ourselves. Sometimes, we even invited it. Not intentionally, of course, but repeated behavior doesn't consider your intentions, it only reacts to itself.

Let's use a simple example. I'm sitting here now writing this book on a Sunday morning in my home office at 6:30 AM. It was my decision to get up and do this instead of sleep in today. My son got up and we played a game of chess. He beat me, as usual. I went back to work on the book. I'm concerned about the book being finished on time for the publisher. I could procrastinate or let a thousand other things distract me from working on it. When the manuscript is due, I could call the publisher and blame it on my family responsibilities, my grandparents needing assistance, or the needs of my team at work. Or, I can decide not to be the type of person who does that. I do everything in my power to turn the work in on time because I signed a contract with the publisher. That's an agreement, a *promise* to deliver something to someone at a specific time. And they paid me in advance for my agreement to do this. If the book is late to the publisher, it's my fault, not my children's or my wife's or those that work with me.

On the other hand, if it's on time, I accept responsibility for that as well. And good things come out of that. In life, we become known for living up to our agreements or for breaking them. In your life, you've got to strive to be someone that people can count on. If you say you're going to do something, you do it. If you don't, no matter *what* the reason, *you* take responsibility for the results. It may seem obvious, but honoring one's commitments and/or taking responsibility for anything less, is not often seen today.

Today, we have people who sue corporations because the coffee *they spilled on themselves* was supposedly too hot and they were burned. Someone recently sued a lawn-mower manufacturer because a man lost his fingers using the lawn mower to trim his hedges. Yes, he actually started the mower, picked it up, turned it on its side, and tried to trim his hedges with it. When this produced the *obvious* disastrous results, he sued the manufacturer of the lawn mower and he *won*. It was determined that the manufacturer should have anticipated such stupidity and put a warning label on the mower.

New recording artists often sign record deals to make several albums, but, if the first one is a hit, they don't want to deliver on their promise to make the other albums for the amount of money they initially agreed on. The same thing happens with people in new hit television shows. Instead of honoring their commitment and being *grateful* for the success, they walk out until renegotiations can give them what they think they deserve. There are athletes who do the same thing. I don't understand this. Didn't they make a promise to do something and get paid for it? Doesn't that mean anything anymore? To a large segment of the population in America, it means nothing. To the best of my knowledge, there hasn't been a recording artist, musician, actor, or athlete who has yet to cure cancer or create world peace, but they certainly want to be paid as if they did.

What I'm saying is that you can easily differentiate yourself today by simply doing what you promise, delivering what you say you will deliver, and accepting responsibility for both your success and your failure. Do this with your wife, your children, your partner, your team, and your friends. Give more than you expect to get in return. Deliver something of value to the prospect or client without the express expectation of anything in return.

## The Two Key Principles of Top Gun

In *Top Gun Financial Sales: How to Double or Triple Your Results While Reducing Your Book,* I outlined the two principles that guide a Top Gun financial advisor. First, you want to focus your attention on making your clients and your prospects *heroes* to the people important to *them.* Second, you want to focus on business that is all three of the following: high margin, high probability, and low risk.

### Making Heroes of Others

If you spend time trying to figure out how you can make your client a hero to the people he or she needs to make happy, you've done something over and above the norm. It's not enough to make *yourself* a hero. That's the wrong path to go down.

This focus on your part helps you to ask clients the right kinds of questions as you get to know them. If you're trying to figure out who they need to make happy and impress, it will lead you to naturally ask questions that dig beneath the surface of the financial relationship you are beginning to share. You need to get to the truth about what is important to your clients. *Their* needs are what is important. Not yours. Other advisors probably aren't asking the kind of questions that uncover the real family or business situation in which your client operates. Keeping your clients heroes to the people who are important to them will ultimately make *you* a hero to your client.

### Margin, Probability, and Risk (MPR)

The MPR factor is an important criterion to have when you begin to prospect. The ideal client is one who is likely to be high margin and likely to do business with you and your firm, who values you, and who because of their experience and their expectations presents an opportunity to do low-risk business. During booming bull markets, everyone is looking to their financial advisor to make them rich. But booming bull markets don't last forever, and the reality is we may not see one like that experienced in the late 1990s for many, many years. Historically, the markets are nothing like what we have experienced for the past 15 years or so. Markets have returned to normal. In these more ordinary times, people pay you to protect their assets and derive a reasonable rate of return on their money.

When you find the two or three business lines you want to represent to the market, business lines that not only address your strengths but are aligned with the strengths of the firm, make sure they have all three of the following characteristics: high margin, high probability, and low risk. Let me explain.

**High margin.** Margin is a measurement of profitability in any endeavor. A high-margin client is one that does significant business with you, is considerate of your time, respects and values your advice and guidance, and is willing to pay you fairly for it. This is the type of client you desire. When you prospect, it's important to determine if the potential client is the type of person with whom you really want to do business.

The other day, I was talking to J.W., a financial advisor I know fairly well, and he told me that he had recently driven all the way to Alabama, met with a prospect, and got the man to sign the papers and agree to doing business with him. This man had a $1.6 million account and probably would do $20,000 a year in gross revenues with J.W. On the way back, J.W. mulled over how the meeting went in his mind and realized that the guy really wasn't the ideal client. In fact, he wasn't even close. He expected an enormous amount of J.W.'s time and advice, his expectation for returns was way out of line, and J.W. just knew that no matter what he did for this guy, in the end, he would probably get upset over one bad trade and leave. J.W. ripped up the paperwork and called the fellow to apologize. He explained that he had thought he had the bandwidth to handle another account, but then realized how he wouldn't be doing the client a favor by bringing him in and being unable to devote the necessary time and resources to his account. Strangely enough, this made the guy want J.W. as an advisor even more. He insisted that he would give J.W. more money, he would refer his friends, and that J.W. simply needed to get rid of some other client. It wasn't his intention, but J.W. did what we call the *take-away*. This is where you go into the prospecting call or presentation and half way through it, if the person you're meeting with is giving you a really hard time asking questions simply for the sake of asking them, you simply close your briefcase, stand up, shake the person's hand, and say something like, "We're not for everybody. I've enjoyed our time and our chat together. Thank you very much." If the person stops you before you get out the door, usually by saying, "Wait a minute," that's when you know you've got him or her. It's an old technique, but I've seen it done very effectively to turn the tone of the meeting into something that is serious, to let the prospect know that you're not fooling around, that you're busy, and that you've had enough of the nonsense.

Back to J.W., however. How many of us can say that we would have done the same thing with a $1.6 million account, particularly in today's market? I applaud him for his ability to see the value in turning down business that wouldn't leave him with enough time or energy to work efficiently for the great clients he does have—and *could* have. J.W. saved himself and that prospect a lot of time and grief. When prospecting, find out how much the prospects are paying the street and what their expectations are, in terms of performance as well as in the time and other services they demand of a financial professional. You can often find this out by simply asking what they don't like about their current situation, or asking what they would change, if they could, about their current situation.

High probability. When talking about probability as it pertains to prospecting, the Top Gun goes after business that he or she has a high probability of landing. The business you're prospecting for should have a natural home at your firm; it should be in line with the firm's strengths and *your* strengths. If your fees are competitive and you are knowledgeable, the odds of your getting the business are higher.

Too many of us see an opportunity with a large amount of assets attached to it or a large commission, and we get excited about that without asking ourselves one vital question: Can I effectively compete for this type of business? Will the time I spend chasing this opportunity more than likely pay off? If so, when? Who will pay me, when will I get paid, and how much? If the business is one in which you truly have a shot, then you should go for it. If not, your time should be spent looking for business you and the firm have a higher probability landing.

For example, I have an area of expertise in the cash management area. Ten years ago, I was able to parlay this knowledge into a situation that paid me well. As the banks have moved into the business, they have tied the lending side of the business into the cash management side, essentially demanding the cash management business as a condition of the lending business. Am I sore about this? I don't think it's right, but there are many things in this world that aren't right. I've had to adapt to the reality that unless I work for one of the banks that lend my clients money, I have a lower probability of landing cash management business. That's just the way it is.

Our firm, however, is exceptional at executing a particular type of derivative transaction. As a result, I've learned how that trade works and I market it to the same clients I normally would be calling on for cash management business. While doing this, I can always stay in touch with the cash management situation and see if anything changes. An opportunity may arise for me to gain that business back on the merits of our ability to manage money better than the other guy, not lend it.

The fact is, it has been shown that salespeople spend 60 to 65 percent of their time on prospects that are low-probability leads or on clients that don't provide high-margin business. Top Gun simply reverses this number. Sixty to 65 percent of a Top Gun's time is spent on high-margin clients and on seeing high-probability prospects to add to the business. The goal is to spend nearly 100 percent of our time talking to or presenting to people and/or corporations that have a high probability of becoming high-margin clients. To do that, you have to leverage your time. You need to have an assistant or an associate prescreen/pre-qualify the leads you call and/or the people you see.

It's important to develop a system of identifying, contacting, meeting, and closing prospects that will drive your business, not hold it back or keep it stagnant. If your average client has $250,000 in assets, then you need to be looking for the client that has $1 million. If you've trimmed your book according to the Top Gun method, and the top 50 to 100 relationships you are left with as your primary accounts do an average of $5,000 in fees per account annually, then you need to be prospecting people who are paying their advisor $30,000 annually, or more. You need to get your existing 50 to 100 relationships to give you more money to manage, give you more of the business they are already doing with the street. You must grab market share. Grabbing market share is how you grow in down, tough, declining markets. It's how any business continues to grow when the number of customers is shrinking, like we experience from time to time as the market cycles and people step out of the market, step aside, wait. Tell clients you are focusing your business on just a few important relationships, and as a result, you can devote your time and efforts to them unlike anyone else they are dealing with. Show them that doing business with fewer advisors historically has been shown to reduce confusion and duplicative efforts, improve performance, and save money. This will give you an opening to ask for more business. You already have their trust. Now show them how good you can be in *other* areas, serving a wider spectrum of their needs or simply handling more of what you're already doing for them. It makes sense to prospect within your own book first, doesn't it?

**Low risk.** You can choose to do any number of things with your business. Some carry a high level of risk to them, some a low level of risk. Cash management is a good example of a low-risk business. You're dealing with sophisticated professionals as clients, buying and selling lower risk securities within the confines of an approved investment policy set by the client. If you do make an honest mistake in this type of business, it isn't usually catastrophic to the client, nor would you find your career in jeopardy over it. If, on the other hand, you trade options speculatively for a 75-year-old widow, you may find that business financially rewarding. However, it carries a high degree of risk for the client and for you, despite her level of sophistication, her experience, or her net worth.

# CHAPTER THREE

# THE TOP GUN MODEL—RULES OF ENGAGEMENT

*Performance, and performance alone,*
*dictates the predator in any food chain.*

NAVY SEAL TEAM SAYING

## Never Have More Than 50 Relationships

This is the very heart and soul of Top Gun. In order for the model to work, the 50-MAX rule has to be maintained in some form. This means dropping a large portion of your client list. I'm talking about the part that is taking up a great deal of your time and effort without enough payback. You've got several options for handling the downsizing of your book in terms of the number of clients you handle. You can give those clients to a junior broker on your team, put them up for grabs at your office, or even give them to another broker altogether, with some sort of sharing arrangement.

The fact is, many advisors out there have 3,000 accounts that may represent 1,000 relationships. I realize that you may not be very exited about dropping 2,000 relationships that do pay you something, but the mathematics are still the same for you as they were for me. You will probably find that 2,000 of those relationships are paying 20 percent of your revenue. If this isn't true, then you are unlike almost everyone in this business, because the 80/20 rule applies to 90 percent of us.

One way to handle this requirement of Top Gun is to simply build a team around yourself. You should have no more than 50 relationships per registered member of the team. Bring on one or two junior partners, assess their personalities and capabilities, and begin transferring the responsibility of communication and other matters to them. My personal insurance agent has so many clients he has something like seven junior associates handling all of us, and he divides us up alphabetically. If you call his office, you get a message, "If your last name begins with the letter A through C, please press one . . ." and so on. Very impersonal, but when you press your number, the phone is directed to the person who has your account responsibility. It's efficient, though I don't like it because it's so impersonal, but you get the point. You have to be on top of the highest paying clients in the book, you have to go to them and prospect them for more money and more referrals, and you have to be able to honestly tell them that you've restructured your business so that you have essentially given away the majority of your clients so you can concentrate on their needs. With a book of 3,000 accounts, you can probably handle it efficiently with a partner, a junior partner, and one or two registered assistants. Add to that team a dedicated investment analyst—someone who is responsible for doing the account analysis, asset allocation work, presentations, financial plans, market monitoring, and special assignments, and you have a strong base for a team that can do several million annually in revenue, if you apply yourselves.

## The Relationship Tree

It is critical to understand that having 50 relationships does *not* necessarily mean you have only 50 accounts. Fifty relationships can mean 250 accounts or even 500 accounts. We often open up a relationship with five accounts. You shouldn't drop anyone who is somehow connected to an important client. For example, I have a great client—a Mr. *Big*—who owns a very successful business. Because of my relationship with him, I was asked to take on the account of his administrative assistant. Her account is not a large one. Still, I don't drop her because she doesn't do a lot of business with me every year. She is one of the branches on Mr. Big' relationship tree. The whole tree is the relationship and counts as only one. In other words, you just shouldn't be handling more than 50 trees. But those 50 trees could consist of many different people and many accounts.

Likewise, we handle a number of public company executives. Every executive at that company, and all its employees who may work with us and have accounts with us, are one relationship. In a case where we have 20 or 30 individuals as clients within one company, each with two or three accounts, you may be able to handle only ten such relationships before you're at capacity and need to add another team member.

## Bring a Higher Level of Thinking to Your Clients

After you've trimmed the client list or restructured your business in the right manner, you may feel a bit exposed. You may think, *what have I done?* This is just mental bullshit. It's your mind being uneasy about change. Try to remember that change is good. Change is reality. Change is growth. You'll be surprised at the freedom you feel once you get past the mental crap that's holding you back. You must discourage any desire you have to return to those clients who were sucking the life out of you for so long just because it feels comfortable. You want to feel uncomfortable right now. That feeling is going to get you out meeting people, talking to your best 50 relationships and prospecting for more like them or even better. Remember that first month you were on the job in this business? Remember that feeling of desperation? Got you hustling, didn't it? You want to have that feeling again. It was that feeling that got you up in the morning and got you out meeting people.

Another way to look at this is that the chances are pretty high you would eventually lose one of your really big relationships because of the time you spent trying to keep happy the clients at the bottom of the list. Isn't that stupid? Why risk losing your best clients trying to keep the others happy? This is not to say that small clients don't need or deserve money management. They have as much right to proper money management as anyone else. But not by Top Guns. Unless they're branches on one of your 50 trees, leave the smaller relationships to the junior brokers. Only get involved when it's absolutely critical.

Now, the first thing you've got to do once you've cleaned house is to meet with each and every one of your remaining customers face to face. It's important to explain to them what you've done and why you've done it. Say something to the effect of, "I just made a decision to voluntarily restructure my business. I've given a good number of my accounts away. I came to a point where I realized that I could do so much more for *you* and the other clients who can truly use the firepower of the firm, and my capabilities, that it didn't make sense for me to spend my time and the firm's time working with people who can't make use of all that we have to offer. We simply can't be everything to everybody; that is a recipe for failure. If it happens that I take a small financial hit for a little while, so be it. My life will be far more enjoyable if I know I'm doing everything I possibly can for fewer clients than it has been for a while now, doing everything I could *squeeze in* for all the clients that used to be in my book. I'm now in a position to devote much more time to your financial affairs, both personal and business. I want to do more for you. This is a positive opportunity for you and for me. My commitment is to provide you with a higher level of thinking and a higher level of service, which will hopefully result in making and saving you more money. What do you think?" Then shut up and watch what happens.

When I did this, my clients responded in a big way. My assets initially dropped by over 70 percent. But, after I stated my case to each of my remaining clients, my assets began to climb. In fact, they went up 2,000 percent, to nearly $350 million over the next three years. My production soared into seven figures. And this happened during the worst downturn in our industry since the Great Depression.

Another financial advisor I know, who was already doing well into the seven figures, happened to spend some time with me a couple of years ago. I outlined the business model and rules of engagement behind Top Gun to him one day. He very seriously told me that he was going to do everything we had discussed. It made me more than a little nervous when he cut all his clients except for ten. I didn't recommend *that*, and told him so right away. But, this guy knew his business and felt he could get away with it because he had ten relationships that were really, really large. Would you believe that his production tripled in one year?

I wouldn't advocate this approach for everyone. His results were due to the very large institutional accounts he already enjoyed as clients. Nothing in my previous book, this book, or any book is right for everyone. But the evidence is there and the results are compelling. The thinking, strategies, tactics, and methods in Top Gun have been around for a long time. Most people in our business have just stopped using them. People have forgotten how to prospect. Large producers have been culling their book each year and building teams around themselves for years. This isn't new. It was simply time for someone to put the methods down in a way that motivates us to use them. Recent industry circumstances have made it imperative that you do something if you want to stay in the industry and grow your business profitably. That ought to be motivation enough.

## You're Never Too Big to Prospect

Every top producer you ever talk to will agree on one thing: Never, never, *never* stop prospecting. It doesn't matter whether you're a $250,000 producer or a $20 million producer, you always prospect for new business. The number one reason to keep prospecting is that it keeps you sharp. It makes you aware of competitive dangers and a changing landscape in the market in which you operate. The other reason is to consistently upgrade the quality of your 50 best relationships.

Prospecting keeps you both confident and humble. When you're calling on new people every day, you get everything from total acceptance to total rejection. Every once in a great while, it will all seem too easy. You'll call a prospective client. He or she will agree to see you right away and sign on the dotted line before you have time to say, "I love this job!" Of course, there are other times when you'll be told to get lost in no uncertain terms. At no time in my career have I had every call go the way I planned it or visualized it, but that's the exhilaration of the process. That's the game and the fun. Try this sometime. Make a call and go into it with a simple opened-ended question like, "Tell me what you've been thinking about lately." It doesn't even have to be a question structured around your business, the prospect's business or investments, or the reason you gave for coming to see him or her. Just let the person you called lead you. People will often take you to the very heart of what is on their minds. They may tell you their deepest fear surrounding investing. And what valuable information that will be as you go forward with this person! You'll be surprised what you can find out if you just ask an open-ended question like that—and then shut up, listen, and let them tell you how you can help them. If they look at you and tell you how great everything is, then you have some work to do to uncover their pain.

The other day, I went into the office of a prospect who had no idea why I was coming. I had simply set the meeting through his assistant. He is one of the most powerful and connected men in our city. Everyone knows him. The first words out of his mouth were, "I have absolutely no idea how I can help you or why you're here." Sounds like a bad start, right? I loved it. This is the game! This is where the fun of what we do comes in. I was in his office for over two hours! At the end, he gave me his mother's trust fund account, which was being mishandled and overcharged. If I hadn't hung in there and talked to him about just about everything other than investments, this wouldn't have happened. Look around the office. See what the prospect loves to do. It's all there on his wall, on his credenza. How many kids, the planes, the boats, the sports he loves, the people he admires, the awards he's won, the associations he's a member of, the universities he's attended. In ten seconds, I can walk into an office and give you a profile of the person who works there. This is what you need to do. Get good at it. My mentor taught me to do it when I was twenty years old. We would go into meetings together and he would make the presentation and I would do all the observing. At first, I wrote everything down, but later, I just took mental notes and wrote them down after I got to the car. Everything matters, and you observe way more than you think you do. What kinds of clothes does he wear? Custom? Off the rack? Shoes? Are they lace up or loafers? Does he have pictures of children, or none? Does he have photos of himself in action, on a boat, in a plane, on the field, with sports or movie celebrities? Suck it all in and note it in your system. Later, you can use the information noted in the system by screening for a word like *boat,* and everyone you've ever met that has a boat will come up in your contact list. Now you can start doing some fun and creative prospecting. In this case, perhaps you see an article about a new boat that has come out. You can highlight the article, cut and paste it into an e-mail, and send it to that group. It takes one minute, but you've just put yourself in front of a number of prospects.

Here's another fun exercise. Let's say you find yourself at a party or gathering where there are a lot of people who are obviously well to do. Naturally, you'd like to have some of them as clients. As you get drawn into a conversation, think of the person facing you as a jukebox. By putting in a quarter, you get a song out of the machine. Instead of a quarter, ask a question. Your question is a quarter. Put a quarter in and see what you get back. When that new acquaintance responds and asks you something about yourself, keep your answer as brief (but friendly) as possible and then ask another question. Put another quarter in and listen to the song that comes out. See if you can do this all night. Your goal is to go around the room and find out as much as you can about everyone you meet and have him or her know very little about you. Here's what will happen. Everyone at that party will say, "I really liked that guy, didn't you? He was really interesting." Why would they say this? They don't know anything about you! That's the point. People aren't interested in you; they are interested in talking about themselves. People like people who are genuinely interested in them. It's human nature. As a rule, people who you've just met don't care

•

about you—they care about themselves and what's on their minds at that moment.

When the rejection level of prospecting gets you down, which it is bound to do from time to time, keep a picture in your mind of a lake that was created by an earth dam. Every call you make, successful or not, is like putting another bucket of water into the lake. Every call raises the water level. Although you may go a month or two or three without anything that looks like success to point to as a result of your efforts, understand that water is more powerful than earth. The buckets of water you're pouring into the lake are working on the dam, applying more and more pressure, until eventually, the dam breaks and the business starts to come in. Usually when it does, it comes all at once and you'll be wondering if you have enough time to take care of all the work for which you've just signed on.

You need to look at your book of business as a constantly changing thing. It should never remain static. You may have clients who leave for reasons that have nothing to do with you. You continually add clients that bring up the average revenue per client of the book. Remember, there is a client out there who will change your life forever. There's a client like that for everyone in this business. You just have to find him or her. I've been through every major financial crisis on Wall Street since 1980, and it doesn't matter if you're in a recession or a raging bull market, your actions remain the same. You prospect. You make the calls. You bring up the value of the book. You talk to people you've never met and find out what's on their minds. You intelligently approach their fears and concerns and their needs and desires with confidence and well-thought-out solutions.

## Sell to the Strengths of the Firm

From 1982 to 2000, the U.S. economy experienced unprecedented growth. From a historical perspective, wealth expanded at unusually high rates. It is unlikely we will see this kind of expansion on a sustained basis for the rest of our lives. During that period, however, Wall Street firms believed the business model of the future for their firms was to be as many things to as many people as possible. They wanted to capture the big investor, the small investor, the investor looking for advice, and the online do-it-yourself-trader. Things have changed.

Today, we face a period in the economic cycle not unlike the business contraction of the 1970s, in which we saw 50 percent of the jobs on Wall Street vanish. In that environment, the firms and people who survived were those who remained financially conservative, stayed competitive, knew how to prospect, and continued to prospect all the time, picking up market share. If we are indeed entering such a period again, and I believe we are, then it makes sense that more and more firms are beginning to realize that they do not have the financial and human resources needed to be all things to all people. Firms are making decisions about how to best allocate resources. This means maintaining business where they can become or have always been competitive, and eliminating other business.

As financial professionals, most of us are paid by fees, commissions, or a combination of the two. Regardless of our method of payment, our income is tied to how well we sell and how many clients we have that pay us for our services. If we want to survive this cycle, we need to figure out which businesses our firms will maintain and which they are likely to eliminate or scale back. The businesses in which your firm is competitive are the businesses you want to represent as a salesperson. This is no time to become a missionary, trying new areas that the firm is unfamiliar with or not already considered a leader.

## Discretionary Business for 80 to 100 Percent of Your Book

Much to my amazement, there are still financial salespeople out there who rely on making sales calls to existing clients before each transaction, trade, or allocation change. Structuring your business this way is bound to disappoint you. I understand that some firms want you to do this for compliance and legal issues. However, if this is your method of operating today for the majority of your business, you cannot scale the business due to the physical limitations of time you will encounter. Most large producers have already discovered this. However, I am surprised to find how many financial consultants continue to operate this way.

Your business must be designed for speed and efficiency. This is a benefit to your clients just as much as it is to you. How can you quickly make necessary allocation changes if you have to make a thousand phone calls in order to do it? When one of your positions goes up 40 percent in one day for some freak reason and you have to take a profit, how can you do that for all your clients at the same time unless you've constructed your business to do just that? If you have to make a thousand phone calls to ask each person if he or she will sell now, who do you call first? Someone has to be last. And it's not efficient. Busy people don't want to be bothered with calls from their broker soliciting a trade. They have a business to run, or something more important they can be doing with their time. They want to hire someone who clearly understands their goals and the parameters of their personal investment policy, and will just take care it. They want regular updates, they want to know how they're doing, and they don't like surprises, but they don't want a call for every little change that takes place in their portfolios.

If you really want to do serious numbers in the retail investment business, you almost have to have a discretionary system in place for managing money for at least 80 percent of your book of business. This can take the form of pure discretion, in which a client has basically given you written authority to trade or make changes for them according to your mutual understanding. It can also mean putting the money to work with outside managers who have permission to manage their portion of the clients' money according to their specific investment style and expertise. Either way, the bottom line is this: If you have to call every client before you execute a trade, in today's market, you look like an amateur. Most of our customers hire us to take direction from them as to their desired results and give us a directive or investment parameters to follow. They don't want us to call them in the middle of the day at their jobs or while they are on vacation to make a decision on whether to sell Hewlett Packard and buy Dell. They didn't hire us to put them on the spot with these decisions.

It may be a good idea to get these investment parameters written down on paper. Obtaining a formal investment policy is a smart way to do business. You can help your client write a good, solid investment policy (just like a corporation or charity would write) for his or her family's investments. The same policy can be used with you and with other money managers the client may have. By engaging the client in this process, you've already gotten a leg up on the other advisors because you've done something they haven't bothered to do. But no matter whether a particular client has other money managers, you need to position yourself *up front* as the person who will be doing X (whatever way you've agreed on to manage your client's money), and that in doing X, you have discretion over the assets. The paperwork for that permission is signed along with the account opening documents. Your clients understand going in that you will be calling the shots on the asset allocation changes (according to their stated objectives, of course) and that in all the accounts you manage, you probably will be doing the same thing. This puts more responsibility on you as the advisor to the account to do right by your clients. Moves you make in the accounts need to be defensible, intelligent, and correspond with research and the clients' objectives. If you make changes to generate business without backup—meaning without economic, fundamental, or technical evidence to validate your moves—you could be vulnerable later, should the account not do well.

## Shorter Sales Cycles

Dr. Herb Greenberg, CEO of Caliper, Inc., and founder of the country's leading psychological testing company, has done a number of studies of the sales process and sales productivity.

His findings are very clear: Regardless of the industry or product being sold, the salesperson with the shorter sales cycle simply does more business.

A short sales cycle starts with excellent screening. By "getting the green lights" before going out on meetings, you greatly reduce "airballs," or meetings that should never have taken place. You greatly increase the probability of meeting with someone who is liquid, has a need for your service, and can make a decision on the spot—or at the very least, within 30 days. When you have to wait over 90 days, the odds of the prospect ever doing business with you fall off a cliff.

A good way to set up a shorter sales cycle is to inform the prospect that you will be asking for a check and an account on your first meeting. I saw this done very successfully by a salesman named Larry Benzie many years ago. Larry was a great salesman. He would call people, book appointments, and as he was getting ready to sign off the call, he would say something like, "Dr. Johnson? Don't forget to bring your checkbook, OK? I'm serious now, Doctor. You're going to like what you see here, so don't forget to bring your checkbook. We're going to want to get started right away."

Larry had kind of a funny voice and he had sort of a natural laugh in the way he spoke. So, even though it may sound outrageous to read it on the page, when Larry said it, it didn't sound offensive. He had a way of making his prospects feel comfortable. He had fun with them. Beyond that, he made them feel enthusiastic about the meeting. When potential clients got off the phone with Larry, I'm sure they wondered whether Larry was serious about having them bring their checkbooks. But just in case, they often did. Larry Benzie was famous for closing deals at the first meeting. Larry depicted the salesman that let you know that he was busy. He had a lot of people to see during the day, but he also made it clear he had something you should want. If a prospect couldn't figure that out during the first meeting, he wished them well and said good-bye.

One of the big mistakes commonly made by salespeople is believing that discussing business with someone over a long period means building a relationship. Wrong. In fact, by not opening an account, yet actively engaging in discussions with the prospect, you reinforce his or her behavior. Soon your relationship is based on a foundation of really warm and fuzzy discourse without any business. You have to remember that you build relationships with *clients*, not prospects. Prospects are nice people, but they deserve *nothing* from you and are entitled to *nothing* from you until the day they become clients.

## One on One, One by One

There just aren't that many business owners or real players in this business who go around to seminars or respond to letters of introduction or other such nonsense. A busy, wealthy person just isn't going to go to a seminar. It rarely happens. Trust me. So I'm not a big fan of doing the seminar thing unless you're truly going into it realizing the clientele you will be attracting.

If you want to do business with the people with real money, you have to pick up the phone, schedule a meeting, and go to see them. State your case, ask them relevant questions, come back with a coherent plan that addresses their needs and desires—then ask for the business. Forget about the seminar scene. See your prospects one on one. Most rich people don't discuss their money needs and wants in front of a group of strangers. As a rule, it just isn't done. In a face-to-face meeting, a potential client will share a lot more information, you can learn a great deal more, and you can get the business done.

## Critical Core Concerns

Every market participant, whether it be a retiree, an executive, a young family man or woman, a new homebuyer, a small company owner, an independent salesperson, a lottery winner, or an inheritor, has one or two critical core concerns. For example, retirees have two simple critical core concerns: income and safety. This is what you take to them. This is what you talk about. This is how you get and hold their attention, particularly on a first call or meeting. This is what you have to show them you can deliver using your firm's strategy or the strategy you designed that your firm is comfortable with and can execute upon competitively. It may seem simple, but people aren't doing it. Why do we see so many people calling on retirees with growth ideas? Why do we come across so many accounts in the hands of retirees overloaded with growth funds and Internet stocks?

Bring some thinking to what you're doing! Who is your market? What are their unique critical core concerns? Are you taking a plan to them that addresses these issues first? Are the accounts you currently work with set up to address the critical core concerns of that client? Sometimes the client or prospect isn't able to verbalize his or her own critical core concerns. You have to do it for them.

TOP GUN: "Mr. Johnson, other retirees I work with have two critical core concerns: income and safety. Would you say that you share these core concerns, or is there something different about your situation that I should know so I don't make an assumption here that is incorrect?"

PROSPECT: "No, you are correct. Those are my primary concerns."

TOP GUN: "Fine. Then I will address these two concerns in the proposal I'm going to talk to you about. Any other matters we can address after we make sure we have these two issues nailed down and you feel secure about those being covered thoroughly, OK?"

You can't do this, however, unless you know the critical core concerns of the market or person you're talking to.

## Diversify into Two or Three Noncorrelated Business Lines

Focus is important for achieving high levels of business. However, to focus exclusively on only one business line can expose you to a high level of risk. Remember the old saying about putting all your eggs in one basket? It's a good one. Too often I've seen producers focused on one investment product who were practically put out of business when the firm decided to leave that line of money management. Municipal bonds in the 1980s is one good example. Many firms who maintained a nice inventory of munis for customers simply decided to get out of that business. The margin of profitability wasn't high enough. A number of producers had no one but municipal bond buyers as their clients. When the inventory vanished, so did their ability to bring product to their clients. These guys were almost wiped out. At the very least, they had to go through years of painfully retooling their business. Some managed it, but others did not. They either left the business altogether or were forced to go to the firms where the municipal bond inventory remained.

The alternative strategy I suggest is to take another look at the strengths of your firm. See in what lines of business it is strong and will likely remain. Drive business to those areas of the firm. Find out what areas of the business the firm wants to move toward in the future. What business lines has the firm been investing in over the past two years and building up? Are they adding people, technology, and capability to these areas? Has it resulted in a rollout of new products or services? How has that rollout gone? Is there a lot of business flowing to that area now? Knowing this information will give you a sense of the direction the firm is interested in moving. Look at the company's annual report and find out what areas of the business produce the most profitability. What areas of the business are achieving profitable growth?

These are the areas in which you want to position your business. Find two or three areas in which the firm has a competitive advantage—a truly deep bench of personnel, experience, reputation, and capability. These businesses are least likely to be at risk of elimination in a downturn. These are the businesses in which the firm will remain despite market conditions or economic cycles because these businesses are what the firm does best. These are the core businesses of the firm.

## Eliminate Negative People in Your Life

One night when I was young, my friend Marty and I were driving from Los Angeles to Orange County down the 405 freeway. All the way, I'm bitching and moaning about this and that, complaining about everything that came to mind. In fact, not a word that came out of my mouth was positive. Finally, Marty pulled the car off the road and told me to get out. I said, "Marty, it's 9:30 at night and it's dark and we're in the middle of nowhere! What the hell do you mean, 'get out!'?"

Marty said, "I made an important decision recently—something good for my life, something so that I can get through this life the way I want to—happy and glad to have lived it. I decided to surround myself with people who are up, positive, and happy about being alive. Which means, I am eliminating all negative people in my life. Right now, you are the most negative person I know. I know this isn't like you normally, Scott, but lately, you've been a real downer. You can make a decision about what kind of person you want to be. If you decide to be a pain in the ass, then so be it, that's your choice. But *my* choice is not to be around you if you are a negative guy. It would be different if you had a particular problem. If that were the case, I'd do everything in my power to help you. But you're just complaining about anything and everything. And I hate that. So, you make the decision—either you're a positive person and willing to see the good side of life, or you can get out of the car right now and best of luck to you."

Ouch—that really left a mark. His words not only struck a cord with me that day, but I've carried them with me ever since. He was right. I had been growing more and more negative. I had been looking at everything from a rotten point of view. He was right about something else, as well. It was *my* choice how I viewed the world, just as it was *his* choice who he allowed into his life. That was a life changing moment for me. There he was, probably my best friend at the time, basically willing to toss me out of the car over my attitude. I don't think he would really have tossed me out of his car that night, but had I not changed my ways, he would have definitely tossed me out of his life, and I knew it. To Marty, attitude was everything. Marty was right.

That was an important lesson. Negative people are downers. They can be terribly infectious, bringing others down with them. Personally, I don't understand how anyone can be negative and be in this business, but they exist. They're in every office, at every firm. What is amazing to me is how many people are negative even when the market is on fire and everyone is making money. How can you be negative in the face of a raging bull market? How could you be negative in a bear market and still come to work every day? I don't understand how people can continue to work in an environment that causes them so much unhappiness.

Negative thinking, complaining, griping, backstabbing— these are the worst cancers that can grow at a firm. If someone has a legitimate gripe, that's one thing. It should be spoken about and dealt with. What I can't stand is when someone complains to everyone and anyone who will listen *except* the boss.

Around the boss he or she will appear to be a first-class cheerleader! You know the type. All offices have (at least) one.

The best thing you can do for yourself is to remove negative people from your life. Once you let them know that you are no longer going to accept that kind of bullshit, you've given them a choice. They can either take heed in what you've said and change their ways, much like I did when my friend Marty woke me up, or they can go prey on somebody else.

Here's how you do it: "Listen, Fred, I think you're a great guy, but you come in here and dump this negative crap on me every day or so, and frankly, I'm not interested in hearing it anymore. What I'm interested in is surrounding myself with positive, upbeat people in every area of my life, and right now, you aren't one of those people. If you have a specific problem that I can help you with, let's hear it. Maybe we can find a solution. But, I don't want to hear you complain on a daily basis anymore. It's hard for me to say this to you Fred, because I think you're a great guy, but unless you get rid of that negativity I don't want to be around you, buddy." Your Fred will either leave you alone or change his or her ways. Either way you win.

## Never Say No for Someone Else

Many times we look at a list of names and automatically start making decisions about whom we should or shouldn't call. Our internal voice will tell us, "This guy wouldn't be interested in talking to me," or "This guy already has a consultant, why bother?" Sound familiar? I still find myself getting caught in the trap from time to time. I call this saying no for someone else. If this is a cold-call list, you don't know the people on it. Chances are you've never even met them, yet for some reason you claim to know what they're thinking. Somehow you have become a mind reader, and you believe there are people on your list who are unlikely to want to do business with you. *Call them.* Never *ever* say no for someone else. Until you hear the word *no,* you're in the game.

After you've met with someone and made your pitch, you may think the meeting didn't go so well and decide not to call back. You imagine that the answer is probably no, anyway, so why bother? There you go again, saying no for someone else. Remember, it's not a no until you hear it directly from the prospect. Instead of hearing something negative you could call and hear something like, "Hey, I'm glad you called. I know I told you in the meeting that I wasn't really interested in pursuing things with you, but over the last week I took a real hard look at my situation. What you said in the meeting make me think. My current consultant isn't giving me what I want and I think it's time for a change."

## Rehearse, Rehearse, Rehearse

All the good performers rehearse tirelessly. All the actors, all the athletes, all the captivating speakers. They know that in order to appear flawless, they have to work through their flaws hundreds of times. As professional communicators, we must do the same. We may not all talk to huge groups of people, but every time we make a sales pitch, we're public speaking. Get in front of the mirror and talk to yourself. See how you look when you present. Years ago the guys in my office and I used to tape ourselves in role-play situations. We'd review the video, rehearse for a couple hours and then tape ourselves again. It's important to practice every possible scenario. You must be prepared for every possibility, every argument.

The purpose of repeated rehearsals is twofold. First, you want to be prepared. The more you talk about something, the more comfortable you are with it. No two prospective clients are going to respond to you exactly the same way. You don't want to get thrown off the track by a response or question you weren't prepared for.

The second reason for repeated rehearsals is so that you appear and sound natural. This is important throughout the sales process—on the cold call, in the presentation, or on the closing conversation. No credible actor or actress sounds like they're reading from or have memorized a script. What makes something real is its authenticity. What you say has to come from the heart. First and foremost, you have to believe in what you're selling. If you don't, find something else to sell—ASAP.

Know what it is that you want to say. Rather than write out an entire script and try to memorize it, make a note of three to five key points you need to make before your call is through. When you role-play with your associates, have them try to get you off the track of what it is you want to say and find out from the person on the other end of the line. Your challenge will be to fit in your key points and extract the information you need in as smooth and natural a manner as possible. This is not to say that you don't listen carefully to your prospects' words. The art of being a great salesperson lies largely in how well you listen and respond to the needs of your future clients. A successful conversation is a give and take of information. If you only give or get information, you won't be successful in your efforts.

The same thing applies when you're talking on the phone. You should have a very good idea where you want the conversation to go. Keeping a set of bullet points in front of you will lessen the possibility of your forgetting to say something crucial. Still, you want the prospect to have the freedom to say what's on his or her mind. There is nothing worse than talking to someone (and this is true about *any* conversation—not just in sales) who isn't listening to what you're saying, but rather listening for you to take a breath so that he or she can jump in and continue with a personal agenda. Let me say it again: Superior salesmanship is a true art form. There is a fine line between too much talk and not enough talk. A Top Gun moves brilliantly above that line, but doesn't cross it.

## Know More Than the Competition

People want to work with people who are smart. This doesn't mean they won't deal with anyone who didn't graduate from Wharton or Harvard, but it does mean that you need to know more than the competition. You will be considered brilliant if you have the information that people want and need. They couldn't care less about the things you know that don't concern them. So, reciting everything you ever learned about corporate investing to a couple who need help with their retirement funds will not make you look smart. Quite the contrary. If you're entering into a conversation about retirement planning, you need to know the rules and regulations cold. You have to know more than their CPA so that you can talk to that CPA and have his or her respect. If you work with corporations, you need to know the concerns specific to that particular type of corporation, the regulations as well as the accounting treatments that may impact it as a result of various recommendations you may make.

Ideally, you want the information you relay to "come from source." This phrase means that your response is instant because you absolutely know the material cold. The information has become like source code in software, imbedded in your knowledge system and retrievable on command. Of course, I did say that's the ideal scenario. Obviously, no one is positive about every answer. Even similar situations may differ slightly. Sometimes, there is more than one interpretation of a law or policy. When incidents like this present themselves, state up front that you don't know the best answer yet, but you will investigate the particular circumstances and get back to the prospect on the matter with your firm's best thinking within 24 hours. Then deliver on that promise. In fact, doing this will actually give you an opportunity to show your prospect exactly what kind of person you are, someone who follows through. Doing this just reinforces that you are someone they can rely on to deliver on their investment portfolio.

If you are a financial advisor to individuals, you must have a methodology that I, or any other competitor, can't blow out of the water. I'll be honest. If I run into one of your clients, I'm going to ask your client about your methodology and how it's working for you. Should I be answered with a blank stare, that tells me you haven't communicated yourself thoroughly. I will take it as an opportunity to state a better case for your client's well-being. It may be that you don't even have a clear methodology for that client. Perhaps you've been together for a long time and the methodology has become one big gray area. Time to tighten that up. It will be good for you and good for the client, and your performance for the client will probably get better.

Let us assume for the moment that you have a methodology and you have communicated it clearly. It better be a good one and I'll tell you why. If your client comes back to me on that question with, "We did a financial plan and an asset allocation model, and we invest the money according to that," you're dead. Why? Because that's not a higher level of thinking. That model has lost people money. That model can be torn apart in two sentences.

Learn about the various methods of portfolio management. Read the studies done by economists that explain why certain beliefs you may have about how companies should be valued and how portfolios should manage risk are no longer valid. Read the reports in the financial journals that are disproving some of the very fundamental beliefs that underlie what we had been taught about risk, reward, valuation, and asset allocation. For goodness sake, if you're really going to be in this business, you should be a student of the business, don't you think?

An example of what I'm talking about is the Efficient Market Hypothesis, or EMH. This hypothesis has been the central proposition guiding finance for three or four decades. It states that security prices always fully reflect the information in the marketplace, and that real world markets like U.S. stocks and bonds are efficient. This has lead to the notion that the average investor (including pension plans, institutions, and so on) cannot hope to beat the market, and is the primary supporting thesis on which the idea of investing in index funds on a no-load basis is built. Why try to beat the market? The market is efficient, therefore, I can do nothing to beat it. As a result, I might as well be passive and just invest, hoping for the best, right?

Wrong. EMH is invalid. Today, probably a hundred studies have been done challenging EMH. Andrei Schleifer, in his book *Inefficient Markets: An Introduction to Behavioral Finance,* said that "in the last twenty years, both the theoretical and empirical evidence supporting EMH have been challenged. New studies of securities prices have reversed some of the earlier evidence which supported EMH." You see, the problem with EMH is that the theory rests on three fundamental beliefs: First, that all investors are rational. Second, if there are irrational investors, their trades are random and cancel one another out. And third, to the extent that investors act irrationally all in the same way at the same time, there are professional arbitrageurs that will step into the market and eliminate any influence the irrational players may have on the market.

Anyone who has delved deeply in the market for any length of time knows that these things are not true. However, it was these beliefs in the 1960s and 1970s that made a superstar out of Milton Friedman. The University of Chicago became the center of the economic and finance universe! This thinking was center stage, dominant, and overwhelming. The work these men have done and continue to do is historic and incredible, but they, as scholars and intellectuals, would be the first to agree that the nature of financial thinking is an evolutionary one. It is natural for new theories to become a big deal in the beginning. A fresh idea is consuming and all encompassing at first. But once that idea settles into the mainstream, as new ideas usually do, it becomes less overwhelming as it relates to our financial and economic thought. Such is the case with EMH.

As Schleifer points out, "To begin with, it is difficult to sustain the belief that investors are rational." Empirical evidence suggests that investors often fail to diversify, chase returns, trade too often, and typically fall into the trap of following gurus. We also know through studies that investors are subject to extrapolation bias, meaning that they rely too much on the past performance of a stock, a company, or a market/asset class to predict future results and performance. "This leads to the overpricing of glamour stocks and lower future returns as they fail to be trees that grow to the sky," says Schleifer. More dangerous for your clients, it can lead to their not getting to their desired result in order to retire or send their kids through college.

When I see the glamour stocks or mutual funds of the day in my prospects' portfolios, I give them the EMH story in an abbreviated form. Then I tell them their advisors have positioned them perfectly for disappointment and failure based on the empirical evidence that exists today. I point out that their advisor is probably still operating under a methodology built on a theory that has been invalidated. In other words, it has a good likelihood of failing without a good dose of luck. I ask them how lucky they feel. If they are feeling real lucky, there is nothing I can do other than bless them and move on. But if they believe as I do, that we may have some tough markets ahead of us, then I'll suggest that they might want to work with someone who has a method in which luck and hope are not a large component of the plan for success. I simply show them another way. Game over. Someone just lost another client.

Knowledge is power. If you know the investment theories of the day, if you know what is valid and what isn't, if you know the arguments on either side of a financial debate and have a thoughtful response and opinion on the matter, you can win business. More importantly, you can avoid making some stupid mistakes and help your clients avoid them as well. You can't do this, however, unless you are truly a student of investment, finance, and economics. To be a student of these matters, you have to love them, otherwise you're just another person doing a mediocre job. Chances are, you'll be average for the rest of your life. *You have to love this stuff.* So if you don't love it, get out now and let those of us who love it go to work for your clients. If you do love it, take it to the next level and become a student. Get better at what you do. Learn what the other guy doesn't know and use it against him to win business and take better care of the client.

## Adjust Your Comfort Zones

How normal does this sound? You come in the office, pick up the phone, call someone you don't know, and ask if it would be all right for you to come over and talk about his or her money. In response, you're told it's none of your business, called a slime bag used-car salesman, and hung up on. You then repeat this activity 50 times before lunch.

*Not normal!* This is simply not normal behavior for grown men and women, is it? Most people are comfortable with talking to their friends and coworkers on the phone. When they have to talk to strangers, there is usually some sort of set-up, so the call isn't a total surprise. Yes, this is how it is with most people, but not for you and me. We've had to completely readjust our comfort zones. We literally have had to reverse what is comfortable for most people. We have to be more comfortable talking to people who don't know us than with people who do. We are so upside down with what is comfortable that sometimes, when we're talking to people who are our friends but who don't have accounts with us, we find ourselves *uncomfortable.* Why? Because they are taking up valuable time talking to us when we could be talking to someone who will swear at us and hang up. *That's* what we've become comfortable with. How's that for weird?

Weird as it may be, when we're talking business, after a day in which you have not been told to get lost at least ten times, you should feel like you didn't give it your all. You are not progressing unless you get a lot of people to turn you down every day. Most people would emotionally fall apart after a short time in our business. They would absolutely break down and cry like little babies. We don't. We like it. Are we sick? Perhaps. But we're successful.

Of course, I'm exaggerating a little bit, for affect. There *is* a difference between friends and clients (this is not to say that the two are mutually exclusive, but I would never make being a client a prerequisite of a friend). The point I'm trying to make is that being turned down is a fact of life in our business. We can't let that deter us. What we have to focus on are the *yes*es. It is not unusual to have to hear 50 *no*s before we hear a single yes. That's our business. But, one yes is often worth all the nos.

## Find the Pain

One of my former colleagues, Mike Conrad, is the master of the "finding the pain" technique of selling. The thinking behind this is simple: Unless the prospect has a feeling that something needs to be fixed in the way his or her money is currently being managed, he or she is not likely to make a change. Think about it. You're proposing to prospective clients, who (for the most part) don't know you from Adam, that they sever their relationships with other people and put their faith in you. You want them to believe right off the bat that their financial future is safe in your hands. We have pretty high expectations of our prospects, wouldn't you agree? Mike knows that the probability of success is much higher if he can locate the areas of pain or discomfort in the prospective client's current situation. He then hammers on that pain, reiterating and confirming its existence over and over again until the prospect is practically writhing in agony. At this point he provides them with the solution that eliminates the pain, saving the day. The prospect is so relieved to have the problem solved that he or she gratefully jumps on board. This is a highly effective technique.

## Fill or Kill Often

The phrase *fill or kill* is used in trading for an order that you send to the floor immediately. That means, in essence, either the order is filled right now, or it is killed on the spot. In or out. Either way is fine, but nothing in between is acceptable. The abbreviation for this order is FOK.

In prospecting, we talk about FOK as it relates to the reaction from your prospective client. Assuming that you're making *a lot* of calls and asking each prospect for a face-to-face meeting, you don't have time to waste while someone jerks you around, offering every excuse under the sun as to why a meeting should wait. Everyone you come in contact with is asked for a meeting, one on one. Either they are willing to book a time for a meeting with you right away or take an intermediary step such as faxing you a copy of their current investment statement, or *you* will have to forgo that opportunity at this time. When a person puts you off right from the very beginning, chances are that he or she was *never* going give you a nickel. I cannot reiterate this strongly enough. When people are unwilling to see you face to face or take a step in your direction prior to a meeting, the chances of them *ever* becoming a client are small. Move on.

If you have called someone and he or she has asked you to call back, then you should make that return call. Sometimes, the timing is legitimately off, but the interest is sincere. When you do call back, your call should be taken and the prospective client should engage you in conversation. This conversation is critical. You want to find out if he or she can meet you face to face. You should already know that this client is qualified. Hopefully, the meeting will be scheduled. If it is put off again, asked to be faxed a financial statement or an investment accounts statement, explaining that when you do meet, you can be more effective in the ideas you bring to the table. If a prospect is unwilling to take this step, don't reschedule. Don't call again. Drop it and move on. There are too many people out there who truly do need your help and will value your services for you to waste time on flakes.

## Things to Remember about a Top Gun Producer

A Top Gun producer:

- Accepts responsibility and owns his or her performance

- Chooses to be positive rather than negative

- Seizes opportunities in tough markets

- Gets closer to clients while others see clients' defects

- Never, never, never stops prospecting

- Brings a higher level of thinking to clients

- Is a leader to his or her clients

- Meets prospects face to face, one on one, one by one

- Does not compromise his or her integrity or business philosophy

- Takes care of his or her internal allies

- Responds when others reach out for help

- Forgives, but never forgets

- Lives by the code of Wall Street since it began, "Your word is your bond."

- Is clear about his or her mission and objectives

- Is prepared

- Maintains a short sales cycle

- Never has more than 50 client relationships

- Has a focused, yet diversified, business

- Sells to the strengths of the firm

- Is not content to be average

- Is well rehearsed and knows the topic

- Is a low-cost, high producer

- Is fiercely protective of his or her three most valuable assets: time, reputation, ideas

# CHAPTER FOUR

# THE MATHEMATICS AND PSYCHOLOGY OF PROSPECTING

*Do not worry about your difficulties with mathematics.*
*I assure you mine are far greater.*

ALBERT EINSTEIN

## Mathematics

Some believe that prospecting, and in fact all success in sales, is based on a mathematical equation. Nick Murray, the author of *Gathering Assets* and a regular financial columnist, defines the mathematical equation for prospecting as 1/n. His theory is that prospecting is *purely* mathematical. According to Murray, 1/n means that you will get 1 client for every *n* calls you make. If you make 100 contacts and you get 1 appointment out of that 100, your equation is 1/100, or 1 percent. He says that this is the "basic law of the universe of prospecting that you and I live in" and that "once you settle into your optimum style of prospecting, there isn't much you can do or say to change *n*." It is his belief that your success is determined *not* by whom you called, what you said, or how you said it, but solely on the number of prospective investors you spoke with. No offense to Mr. Murray, but I think he is only half-correct. Here's why.

If he is right and prospecting is purely mathematical, then why do some people make 20 or 30 appointments for every 100 contacts and others make only one or two? What explains that? The only answer is the person with a higher level of success is calling more qualified people, is talking about the right things, and talking about them the right way. There is no question in my mind that in successful prospecting it does matter who you call, what you say, and how you say it. It matters a lot.

Now, the very valuable lesson in Murray's book is that we should put rejection in the right perspective. He's trying to let us know that we're going to be rejected and that we shouldn't take it personally. This is true. He's trying to tell us that we need to talk to a lot of people. This is also true. And by the grand law of averages, it is logical to expect that the more contacts you make, the greater your chances of landing a new client. In my opinion, this is more an outcome of common sense than it is a mathematical equation or breakthrough.

Murray admits that $n$ is a number that will differ for everyone. I agree. However, this again begs the important question, why is $n$ a small number for one person and a large number for someone else? The answer to that would be truly useful information, right? If he could tell me how to change $n$ from the 100 contacts I have to make to get one appointment, to only 10, *that* would be something I could use. That would help me succeed.

Top Gun will improve the mathematics of prospecting for you. It's where we change $n$ to a lower number, to put it simply. We do that using creativity, knowledge, and a decent understanding of human behavior. I call it the psychological art of prospecting. And a good artist can take the number $n$ from 100 down to 10 using what we know about how humans react to certain things, certain words, certain phrases.

Top Gun looks at prospecting as a probability formula. Our business is all about probabilities. You have to find a way to do business so that the probabilities are in your favor, and apply at every level of this business every day. If success in prospecting was just about the number of people contacted, what would be the point of perfecting your pitch? Why bother to educate yourself on all the different options available in money management? Why would you even listen to what a prospective client wanted? All you'd have to do is keep calling people. If you or a computer made enough calls, your success would be imminent! We know this is not true because we know people in our own offices who dial the phone 200 times a day and get not one good contact. Eventually, that person will quit because that's too hard. A human being can only take so much, right?

Nirvana would be making an appointment with every call. But that doesn't happen—not to *anybody*—because of circumstances that we can't control, such as the prospects' attitudes or moods, the prospects' prior experiences with financial advisors, the prospects' current financial situations, and the prospects' schedules. If you want to make prospecting an equation, you have to include these factors.

Another part of the equation is the circumstances we *can* control. We can control who we call, what we say, and how we say it. We can also control how well we know our business, how creative we can be in our pitch, and our ability to listen. We can control our reaction to people's moods, as well as our own dispositions. We can take steps to improve all of these things. We are not computers, which is to our advantage.

If, for fun, we were to try to base our business on a mathematical formula, it really couldn't be as simple as the number of calls you make that determines the number of appointments or clients you obtain. That wouldn't be accurate. Let's look at the equation a little differently by first determining what factors are within our control and what factors are outside of our control.

Group A consists of factors over which we do have control:

- Who we call ($w$)

- What we say ($s$)

- How we say what we say ($ss$)

Group B consists of the factors over which we don't have control:

- The real financial condition of the people we call ($f$)

- Their mood at this moment ($m$)

- Their attitude towards money and investing, or previous experiences with financial advisors ($a$)

- Their schedule ($s_3$)

If we were to write an equation for the probability of prospecting success, where success (S) is defined as lowering the number $n$ in the equation $1/n$, then it could look like this:

| | A | | B |
|---|---|---|---|
| | Controllable Factors | | Noncontrollable Factors |
| S = | (w+s+ss) | × | (f+m+a+$s_3$) |

where in Group B, the maximum value of any factor is +1 and any negative is -4; and in Group A, the maximum value of any factor is +3.

For example, say you call a wealthy business owner in a good mood, great attitude, and open schedule, but you haven't worked on Group A skills. In this case, w=3, s=0, and ss=0. Group B=4. Group A=3. AB=12.

Suppose another advisor calls the same business owner, and he or she has worked hard on Group A skills. This caller's W=3, s=3, and ss=3, for a total of 9. AB=36. This advisor's chances of booking an appointment with this great prospect are three times greater than yours.

A negative resulting S is a failure to get an appointment or achieve your goal. If any of the factors in Group B are negative, then the entire equation is negative, but if Group B is positive or neutral, then the cumulative number of the first set of controllable factors, if higher, will result in a higher degree of success (S). A successful call, therefore, will be one in which Group B is a positive number. The number of calls you have to make to positive Group B people in order to get the appointment will be less if you have done everything in your power to have a high number in Group A (the factors you can control) every time you call. So the optimal situation is one in which you have a positive number in Group B and a very high number in Group A.

Because you cannot control the factors in Group B, but you can control the factors in Group A, you can only work diligently and intelligently to increase the number you almost always have within Group A. I call this "optimally structuring the controllable factors." This is simply making sure that you call people who have a high probability of being qualified. On top of that, the things you say to them should be well thought out and designed to get their attention. They should differentiate you from the other twenty calls that good prospects receive from financial people in a day. The way you say what you say is improved through practice, rehearsal, role playing, and actual trial and error in real time on real calls with real prospects. If what you're saying isn't working at all, then you need to adjust. Take note of what people are reacting positively to and make sure you put that into every call. Keep adding these up in a call, and soon you'll have three or four bullet points, concise statements that will elicit the response you want and result in a meeting being set.

This equation gives the appropriate higher power to the uncontrollable factors that can lead to a prospecting failure. This is because any single negative factor in this category (no money, a bad mood, a poor track record with previous advisors) has the power in and of itself to end the encounter, regardless of how well we design or structure the controllable factors.

Before you think I've lost my marbles, stay with me for a minute.

As I said, any one of the factors we cannot control (Group B) has the power to blow all our efforts out of the water and result in a failed attempt. There is nothing we can do about it. It's out of our control. Statistically speaking, we will come across a number of people every day that have a sour attitude, that we caught at a bad time, or that may have had a brutal experience with a financial advisor, broker, or other financial professional in the past. We can't change that. This is why there is no such thing as a 1/n=1, or perfect prospector. So we move on to the next call. You are not a missionary, you are a farmer, and you only go around looking for ripe fruit to pick. You are not put on this earth to change people's religion. If they hate financial advisors, or they just had a fight with their spouse, so be it. Next call!

On the other hand, we are just as likely, in the course of any given day, to come across people who are neutral or positive on the factors outside of our control. When this happens, the outcome of the equation lies *within* the things that we can control. This is when two things matter: what you say and how you say it. What you say and how you say it differentiate your results from those of others in prospecting or cold calls.

The other day I had scheduled a meeting in Florida to see a prospect that had already agreed to become a client over the phone. We had made a plan for him and were going down to present it and sign papers to transfer his accounts to us. In the interest of maximizing our trip, we downloaded a list of prospects in the ten mile radius of our meeting, scheduled the whole day there, and started calling to fill up the appointments for that day in that town, making it a model city for us. On one of the calls, the owner of a consulting business said, "I get a 100 of these calls every week, but something tells me not to blow you off. I don't know why, just something tells me I should see you." That's it. That's the magic you're looking for, and it doesn't happen unless you're calling the right people, saying the right things, and saying it the right way.

What we ultimately want to accomplish is to get as many appointments with prospects as possible in order to turn those prospects into clients. We have to do everything within the realm of possibility to increase the odds of this happening. If we make 100 contacts, we want to make twenty appointments. The guy next to us will be lucky to make one. He may have the same list of prospects, he may be calling at the same time of day, in the same part of the country from within the same firm. What makes you and me different than someone else? The answer lies in the next section: Human psychology and behavioral response.

## Human Psychology and Behavioral Response

Studies have been done in the psychology of sales that prove there are certain things we can say to people that will elicit a particular kind of response. However, we didn't need a psychological study to tell us that. We know there are things we can say or do that will almost always get a specific response. If you were to hide behind a door and scream "BOO!" at the top of your lungs when someone came through the door, you could pretty much guarantee that you'd get a particular reaction. If you told someone they looked like crap today, chances are that person would be insulted. Of course, these are obvious examples. More sophisticated studies prove that even subtle phrases can elicit a similar response 70 to 80 percent of the time.

In Robert Cialdini's book, *The Science of Persuasion,* he tells us about something called *fixed action patterns.* A fixed action pattern is a pattern of action that is set in motion by a trigger feature. These trigger features can either be words, sounds, actions, or colors. When the female of a certain type of bird shows its blue feathers, a mating ritual is triggered in the male. It's almost as if a tape-recorded response is activated inside his head whenever he sees those blue feathers. This automatic reaction is programmed into the bird and the response is the same virtually 100 percent of the time.

These fixed action patterns occur in humans as well. It's like when you're driving down the highway and you hear an old song on the radio and it instantly transports you to a time on the beach with a certain person. You can almost smell her perfume and can't help but find yourself smiling. Fixed action patterns can trigger powerful responses and your knowledge of their existence can be very useful. Cialdini sites a study done by Harvard social psychologist, Ellen Langer, showing that people will have a much higher propensity to acquiesce when asked for a favor if they are given a reason for doing so. Positioning herself in a long line of people waiting to use a library Xerox machine, Langer asked the people in front of her if she could cut in line to use the copy machine. Without providing a reason, only 60 percent of the people were willing to let her cut in. It did show that most people, when asked to do someone a favor even without a reason, do want to help. However, when she coupled the request with an explanation ("because she was in a hurry"), some 94 percent of the people allowed her to skip ahead. Wanting to see if the word *because* was what triggered the change, she took the experiment a step further. Eliminating the fact that her original reason was something most people could relate to—being in a rush—she tried saying something ridiculous, "Excuse me, I wonder if I can ask you for a favor. May I skip ahead of you in line because I have to make copies?" Her reason wasn't even a good one—*everyone* in line was there to make copies—but still 93 percent of the people allowed her to go ahead of them.

Having a reason for asking the favor is what was relevant. What that reason was didn't seem to matter much at all. The study didn't end there. Langer tried again, saying, "Excuse me, may I skip ahead of you in line because my Aunt Mary is named Mary?" Still a 93 percent success rate. People simply like to have a reason for doing something, even if it makes no sense. Using the word *because* gives an action purpose. It triggers a fixed action pattern response.

We can use this knowledge in a cold call. When asking for an appointment, supply the prospect with a reason. For example, you might say, "Mr. Johnston, why don't we get together some morning for a cup of coffee before work, *because* I have something interesting to talk to you about and it won't interrupt your schedule?" Or, "Mr. Johnston, why don't we meet some morning before work at your office, *because* that would be more convenient for you." Well, the fact that it would be more convenient for Mr. Johnston is obvious, but when it is stated as a valid reason for getting together, it sets off the tape in Mr. Johnston's head. He is much more likely to agree to a meeting than if you just asked, "Mr. Johnston, why don't we get together for a meeting at your office." Can you hear the difference? If you don't believe this works, give it a try and do your own study. We tried it in my office and found amazing results. You'll be surprised at how much easier it is to get an appointment with three, four, or five people a day simply by using this knowledge of human fixed action behavior patterns.

I cannot stress enough how important it is to perfect the skills that you can contribute to a successful call. Let's look at them again, one by one, and see if there is more you can do to increase your prospecting effectiveness.

## Who We Call

Nick Murray says there is no magic list. He doesn't see the value in *who* you call, but rather in *how many* calls you make. *Garbage.* Come on! Does this mean it wouldn't be wiser to research the names of successful business owners rather than to simply call random names from the phonebook? Does this mean we can't expect to find a different level of success in contacting people who live in an affluent residential area than by contacting people who live in the ghetto? Are basic filtering choices such as these irrelevant to our success? I don't think so. Personally, I'm for working smarter, not harder. By creating or purchasing a quality list of people to call, you lessen the opportunity for disappointment and heighten the possibility for success.

There are certain things you can infer about a person if you have the right information. For example, 90 percent of all business owners who have owned and operated their businesses for more than 15 years, and have more than 50 employees, have at least $2 million in investments outside of their business. If you know this to be true, and you can screen a list for that information, then there is a good chance that at least 90 percent of those business owners you call are going to be financially qualified. You know the chances are high that you'll be talking to someone with $2 million or more. If the guy next to you will be talking to people without a nickel 90 percent of the time, who is more likely to succeed? Who you call does matter.

The real wealth in this nation resides in the business owner that is under everyone's radar. He or she has a business that isn't glamorous, doesn't get newspaper attention, does very well in a certain niche, and is really rich. This person owns his or her own building, and doesn't like debt unless it is used as a tool to increase profitability, but never wants to rely on it. This person owns a house free and clear, has another one or two homes, and when he or she sells a business, will be worth many millions. You find this person by driving out to the office or plant in the industrial part of town, walking up to the door and introducing yourself. You get to this client by doing the extraordinary things that most people will not or cannot do.

## What We Say

Prescreening who we call doesn't provide a *guarantee* of success, it only increases its probability and therefore increases the efficiency of the time we spend in the endeavor. Time is one of our only assets, so the efficient use of it is critical.

With the many prescreening techniques available today, such as Bloomberg, you can be fairly secure in reaching a financially qualified target. But there is no way to be absolutely certain until you've talked to the prospect. Just because you reach someone on the phone who is financially qualified doesn't mean he or she will give you the account. It's possible that the money in question is already in the hands of one or more financial managers. You must get this prospect's attention. You need to make the prospect realize that it is in *his* or *her* best interest to meet with you face to face. You have about ten seconds to make a good first impression.

What are you going to say? That really depends upon the profile of the people you're calling, your target market. If you've done your research, you'll have some background with which to work. Remember that your prospective client is only interested in what you know *as it pertains* to him or her. To hear about anything else is a waste of his or her time, much as you may enjoy talking about what you know. What your prospective client wants to talk about is himself or herself. Any information you relay about *you* should be relevant to them—their job; their industry; their feelings about the markets, investing, or the economy.

The other day I was calling on a list of people who had recently purchased homes. Our local paper had a listing of the names and addresses of everyone who had purchased homes in the past few months, including the prices of those homes. Can you believe it? This was public information! Here is a list, for which I paid nothing more than the annual subscription of the paper, that gave me the names and addresses of fantastic potential clients. I didn't have to do anything to get this information other than open the paper and read it!

I called the people who bought homes worth $500,000 or more. I congratulated them on their new homes and explained that the reason I was calling was that in my experience, going through the process of buying a home is usually a good time to look at personal finances and make plans for the future. I asked if I could stop by and have a cup of coffee some morning before work, explaining that as a welcome gift, I would provide a complimentary financial plan. If they declined, I immediately changed the subject by asking about their new home. How do they like the place? Were they settling in all right? Did they move in from out of town as my wife and I had done many years ago? People love to talk about their new homes. After all, they just paid a pretty penny, so it's usually a source of pride.

I went on to say that Atlanta has been great to my family and that we love it. I was being completely truthful. Psychology is important when it comes to learning how and why people react the way they do. But, it should be used as a tool to build an honest relationship, not to create a facade about who *you* are or what you have to offer. Still, within the boundaries of truth, it was my desire to change their minds about making an appointment. I wanted to be thought of us a human being rather than a used car salesman. When it seemed appropriate, I said something to the affect of, "Frank, I'm glad you're settling in okay. I want you to know that we'll be able to tell within ten minutes of our meeting whether there is anything I can do to improve your financial situation. If I can't, no problem. At the very least, you'll know someone in the community that you can call if you should ever need anything. How about it? I guarantee it won't be a waste of your time. Should we set something up for tomorrow?"

Remember, when initiating a conversation with a prospective client, to keep in mind the things that matter most to the majority of people:

| | |
|---|---|
| Love | Time |
| Family | Health |
| Job | Feeling important |
| Church | Saving taxes |
| Saving money | Making more money |
| Successful retirement | Security and safety |
| Being respected by peers | Children's education |

These are the things that really matter to most of us. The order of their importance changes constantly throughout our lives, but these are common worries. Listen when someone is talking to you about one of them. Maybe you have a way to help alleviate that worry. Money can't buy love, that's true. Nor can money buy good health. But, money can often buy treatment for poor health. It can solve a multitude of other problems, as well. The one thing that money can provide, perhaps above all else, is peace of mind. And people are willing to pay for it if they feel there is a high probability you can help them obtain it.

## How We Say What We Say

Step One: Read Robert Cialdini's books on persuasion. Step Two: Look at the techniques he demonstrates in his books and see which ones you can apply to your business.

Doesn't it just make sense to use what we already know about human behavior and reactions to certain phrases and words to our advantage? Why shouldn't you incorporate what you can learn from behavioral psychology into your speech patterns, the phraseology of your pitch, the construction of your calls, the nuance of your tone, the words themselves?

Here's a simple example. We all know that people have a tendency to want to belong, right? They want to belong to the right club, they want their kids to go to the right school, they want to be seen eating at the right restaurants and to be seen at the right charity affairs. When you ask someone to meet you, wouldn't it be smart to phrase the question in a manner that gave them the impression they were being invited to join an elite group or club of individuals in their town? How do you do this, you might ask? It takes practice. Everything you say about who you are, who you deal with, why you're calling them, and what you're going to share with them should be phrased in such a way that the tone simply leads them to that belief themselves, without you actually saying the words.

TOP GUN: Mr. Johnson, thanks for taking my call. I'm Scott Kimball with Big Bull Financial. My job is to take care of some of our firm's best customers. My team is seeing a client in your city on Monday next week, and I thought that if you had a moment in the morning, perhaps I could stop by your office, because that would be more convenient for you, and share with you a proprietary investment strategy that we're doing for them. The results have been very strong with low volatility, and these clients have asked us to come and show it to them. I can get in early and we can sit down, just you and I, then I can meet my team over at their offices. Is that all right with you?" If I sense some hesitation on his part, I'll quickly throw in a "No obligation of course, just fifteen minutes in your office, then you and I can follow up later."

In that simple sentence, I let him know that there are other wealthy, important customers of ours in his city who we are going to see. They asked us to come and see them, so this must be pretty good. I'm going to come and see him by himself—he doesn't have to be scared about sitting in front of an entire team, so that's a relief. (Subconsciously the prospect appreciates your sensitivity to that potentially scary situation for a person.) He's thinking: He's coming to my office, so it is convenient. The no obligation statement is simply a play on the free trial offer that advertisers have drilled into us for decades. They have spent millions conditioning us to take advantage of free trials, no ob-ligation trial offers, so all I did was use it. People hear it, and click, whirrrr—the tape starts in their heads. All these things are layered on top of one another in the call and the behavioral re-actions are processing through his mind while I'm talking, and all of them are designed to elicit just one result: a yes answer on his part. I want to make it comfortable for him to say yes to a meeting and feel good about it.

I know this book is about prospecting, but here's an exam-ple that relates to closing. When you want to close someone, don't ask them to "go forward with you" or say "Let's do it, come on." Ask them instead to join you, but ask it this way:

TOP GUN: "Mr. Johnson, I've been doing this for a long, long time. I can tell when our investment strategy truly fits for someone, and this seems to me to fit your needs very well. We're having a lot of fun with this and the people who are joining us now are truly happy they decided to join us. Why don't you join us?"

One simple paragraph. Here's what's going on in his head: *My feeling that this might be the right strategy for me is being rein-forced. For some strange reason, I had a visual flash of people having fun. Others are happy they did this. I'm being invited to join the select group of other happy, fun-loving people who are making money and smiling.*

See how it works? People who join are over here having a good time and making money. People who don't join are over there, on the outside, looking at the people having fun and making money. To which group of people do you think the typ-ical human being wants to belong?

There is nothing underhanded or wrong about this. Retailers have been utilizing their findings about how much people spend per square foot when there is a certain scent in the air or music in the background. When they find the right mix of music, décor, and scent, they use it in all their stores. They use it to drive sales. They are not confused about the business they're in, are you?

# CHAPTER FIVE

# THE TOP GUN PROSPECTING PROCESS

*Everyone is trying to accomplish something big,*
*not realizing that life is made up of little things.*

FRANK A. CLARK

## Using SWOT, the Boston Matrix, and CARVER

SWOT stands for Strengths, Weaknesses, Opportunities, and Threats. SWOT analysis is an effective and useful method that management teams at many forward-thinking companies perform on a regular basis.

Look at your firm. What are the areas of business in which it truly excels? Talk to others inside and outside the firm. Find out what the perception of your firm's strengths and weaknesses may be. Write them down. Those are your firm's strengths and weaknesses, because perception is often reality, particularly if you're in sales. Think about how you can incorporate these strengths into your own business. Can you build a business around the strengths of your firm? Even if there are only a couple of these strengths that you can leverage easily, that's all right. We've already discussed that trying to be all things to all people is an effort in futility. Concentrate on those areas in which you have natural knowledge or a client base.

Just as important as knowing your firm's strengths is understanding its weaknesses. They aren't always as obvious, but every firm is weak in some areas. These are the places to steer clear of in your prospecting. You don't want to spend any unnecessary thought or time on areas in which you're not competitively strong.

Look at the marketplace, your clients, and your region. What opportunities exist in the marketplace? Who is making money? Who would naturally have an interest in those very areas in which your firm is strong and has a superior competitive position? Look at your existing clients. Are they using the strengths of the firm right now? Why not? Have you called them and pointed out that your firm is distinctly superior in these areas and that you'd like to discuss how they can take advantage of that in their own investment practices? Look at your geographical region. Who is sitting in your front yard that would or should be interested in your firm's strengths? Have you contacted these people?

A few weeks ago, I cold called a businessman. He agreed to meet with me. He even offered on the first call that he liked my firm and had tremendous respect for us. We met the next day and he proceeded to tell me that my firm is one of his largest clients. We do business with him in another area. We are very important to him, and, he is important to us, I came to find out. His business depends on really strong financial relationships. There was a time in his business not long ago when there was a bump in the road caused by an unexpected situation that he couldn't have been prepared for. Still, everyone in the banking business cut off his access to capital—except us. Needless to say, I was happy to hear that. This is a dream set up for an appointment. I proceeded as though it were any other call. He may have already been happy with the firm I worked for, but he didn't know me personally. I still had to prove that I wasn't an idiot and that he should open an account and do business me, in my area of the company.

He did, and this has led to very strong relationships between me and others in his company. Once I was in, it was completely obvious that this guy should have been called upon long ago. I can see their building from my office window. I drive by their offices at least twice a day, often more than that! All I could do was ask myself why it took me so long to make the call. Opportunities like that exist for everyone. They're often right in your own backyard. You just have to be the one making the calls. The harder you work, the luckier you become.

### The Boston Matrix

The Boston Matrix is a well-known business tool created by The Boston Group and has been used by management consultants for years to help corporate managers assess their business. Which area should receive further investment and which should be sold or allowed to die? This tool helps to answer those questions. Figure 5.1 shows how the Boston Matrix segments businesses into four groups: Stars, Cash Cows, Dogs, and Question Marks.

*Stars* are businesses displaying high-growth characteristics, in which the company is a leader in the market. These are the

---

**FIGURE 5.1 Boston Matrix**

---

|  | **High**    MARKET SHARE    **Low** | |
|---|---|---|
| **High**<br><br>*MARKET GROWTH*<br><br>**Low** | **STARS**<br>High market share in high-growth markets. Require cash for growth but have strong competitive position and should be invested in. | **QUESTION MARKS**<br>Require a lot of capital for growth, but have not yet gained enough market share to be a highly profitable enterprise. Can become a DOG or a STAR. An unknown. |
|  | **CASH COWS**<br>High market share in low-growth markets. They do not require much capital to maintain their position and their cash can be used for STARS. | **DOGS**<br>Cash loser or cash trap. Weak or no profits. Should be turned around quickly or eliminated. Not candidates for serious investment dollars or resource allocation. |

businesses that should receive capital and resources. *Cash Cows* are profitable businesses in which the company has been a leader, and capital requirements are low in order to continue to produce profits. However, the market is no longer growing rapidly. The profits from these businesses can be and should be invested in Stars. *Dogs* are businesses that are losing money, and the outlook for them is not good. They should be turned around quickly or jettisoned immediately, before they suck too much capital from the enterprise. *Question Marks* require a lot of capital in order to grow, but the jury is still out on what to do with them. They show some potential to become a Star, but if not handled correctly, could just as easily become a Dog.

The financial services business is segmented into a number of business lines that can be stuck into each of these boxes. Of course, not being aware of your firm's strengths and weaknesses or your particular specialty, I'm unqualified to tell you which of your businesses belong in which box. Figure 5.2 shows what the landscape looks like from where I sit now. No doubt that those of you doing business in the areas I categorize as Dogs or Question Marks will differ with me. I assure you, this is for illustrative purposes only. I am not passing judgment on any one line of business. I would, however, encourage you to draw up a matrix of your own and fill in the boxes as you see them. If you are in the insurance business exclusively, you should draw one up that segments insurance products. Look at it to see where your business is coming from. Are you doing most of your business in the areas that are dying? Do you only do one type of insurance? The purpose of this exercise is to get you to think about your business. It may help you determine whether it makes sense to add or delete a line of business you are currently working in, based on its prospects for the future.

## CARVER

The Navy SEALS use a technique called the CARVER matrix to determine which targets they should hit and in what order. Former Navy SEAL Richard Machowicz's book, *Unleashing the Warrior Within: Using 7 Principles of Combat to Achieve Your Goals,* talks about CARVER being a battle-tested "no lose" method of target assessment. I've found it to be a valuable tool in determining where a financial consultant's time is best spent. Too often the excitement of a new product or line of business takes up our time and energy unnecessarily. According to

**FIGURE 5.2   Adapted Boston Matrix**

| | High                        MARKET SHARE               Low | |
|---|---|---|
| **High** | **STARS**<br>Insurance Products<br>Structured Products<br>Hedging transactions<br>Derivative Based Lending<br>Hedge Funds<br>Private Equity Funds<br>Swaps | **QUESTION MARKS**<br>Stock Option Plans<br>Stock Purchase Plans<br>529 Plans<br>Commercial Lending |
| **Low** | **CASH COWS**<br>Consulting<br>Equity/Fixed Income<br>Managed Accounts<br>Cash Management<br>Currency Exchange<br>10b-18 Buybacks<br>Mutual Funds | **DOGS**<br>Trading Accounts<br>Lock Box<br>401(k) Plans |

*(vertical axis label: MARKET GROWTH)*

Machowicz's theory, it is a natural phenomenon. Human beings naturally get exited about new things. We have a tendency to want to believe the next great promise. That's not all bad. Sometimes the next great promise *is* everything it's cracked up to be. But most of the time, we are temporarily distracted from what we know to be worthwhile in pursuit of something that isn't. Using the CARVER matrix is an enlightening exercise in that it strips the emotion out of the decision and simply tells you which business you need to focus on first, second, and third.

Here's how it works. CARVER stands for Criticality, Accessibility, Recognizability, Vulnerability, Effect, and Return. Each target is ranked 1 to 5, with 5 being most important and 1 being least important, in each of the six areas. This means the highest score possible is 30.

**FIGURE 5.3   CARVER Matrix**

| Target | Critical | Access | Recognize | Vulnerable | Effect | Return | Total |
|---|---|---|---|---|---|---|---|
| Insurance | 4 | 3 | 2 | 2 | 5 | 5 | 21 |
| Mutual Funds | 4 | 4 | 3 | 4 | 4 | 5 | 24 |
| Hedge Funds | 5 | 1 | 1 | 2 | 4 | 3 | 16 |
| Trading Accounts | 3 | 3 | 3 | 1 | 3 | 1 | 14 |

In Figure 5.3, we ranked four possible businesses you may be involved in marketing now: insurance products, mutual funds, hedge funds, and trading accounts. In this hypothetical example, all four businesses are producing equal levels of business. Your desire is to figure out two things: First, is there a business line you should cut, and second, how should you really be spending your time and focusing your efforts and resources to have the most impact on your business now and in the future?

Ask the following questions as you go through the process:

- *Criticality.* How critical to my business now and in the future is this product? If I stopped selling this product entirely, would my business be devastated? If I sold more of it, would my business grow?

- *Accessibility.* How easy is it for me to find clients who will buy this product? Can I sell it easily? Do I already have a good knowledge base in this product?

- *Recognizability.* Is this an easy sell, typically? Do most people know about this product already, or is there a long and difficult learning curve associated with it?

- *Vulnerability.* How much effort do I have to go to in order to keep this kind of account? What kind of ongoing time and effort is involved in maintaining a high level of performance with this product?

- *Effect.* If successful in selling this product, what level of impact will this have on my business?

- *Return.* If I spend the time, money, and energy to launch into a sales effort in this area, what will be the payback and when will I be paid?

As you can see by the scoring, most of your time is being spent talking to people about and working on trading accounts (the return on investment is low). Yet, this is not the highest scoring business line. According to CARVER, you should be spending a lot of time on mutual funds because it will have the largest impact on your business now and in the future. Next, your efforts should go into insurance, which is ranked second in the scoring. These are the businesses that matter most because they will have the largest positive impact on your business with the least amount of effort. Instead, you're devoting a lot of time and energy to managing trading accounts and selling people hedge funds.

You can see that CARVER can be used to determine which markets will be best for you to spend your efforts and other resources trying to reach and develop. CARVER will tell you which will have the highest degree of impact for the lowest amount of resources expended. It's all about the efficient use of your resources—time, money, personnel, reputation, energy. Using CARVER will clarify and cut through all the emotional attachments or confusion you may have about various alternative prospects, prospecting methods, and so on.

It is truly important that you do this exercise for one simple reason: Time is your greatest resource. Time is the biggest investment you will make in your business and it has a dollar value. If you are a $400,000 producer, the hour you spend on *anything* nonproductive during the workday costs you and your firm around $200 in pure lost revenue. The true cost is higher because of the long-term impact on your business. If a total of 40 hours a year is spent on a low score CARVER activity, it produces a lower return, much the same as making a large investment in a Dog on the Boston matrix. It just isn't healthy for the long-term prospects for the business. General Electric wouldn't make a huge annual investment into a business that wasn't going to pay off down the line, especially if they had the knowledge up front that this was the probable end result, so why would you? These $200 hours add up. Over the course of a month, the cost of an hour here and an hour there each day on efforts that are not high on the CARVER score can cost you thousands.

## Reaching into Your Market

Once you've found your primary market, or at least think you have, you have to reach into it. There are many methods of reaching into your market and creating business. You can advertise, mass-mail letters of introduction, mail offers or invitations, do a radio show, write a column for the local newspaper, network at trade shows, network with influential people in your community, teach classes or seminars, sit at booths at conventions and home shows, walk door to door, and/or make cold calls. I've done almost all of the above at one time in my career.

My personal favorite is the cold call. I don't like to call it *cold calling,* even though that's what it is. I prefer to think of it as meeting new people over the phone. I like this way of prospecting because it allows you to prequalify the prospect efficiently. Unlike sitting at a trade show or waiting for mass-mail responses, where you have no control over who seeks out your advice, when you make the call, you know whose number your dialing. It saves you an enormous amount time, effort, and money. In the course of any given day, you're going to meet people who give off good energy and people who give off bad energy. By using the telephone, you have an advantage. You can simply thank bad energy people for their time and hang up. You're then free to call someone else. You don't get that option at an event or cocktail party. I discuss cold calls in greater detail in Chapter 6.

Once you've decided on the market you want to go after, you need to gather names. Even if you already have a few people in mind to contact, it is smart to get a handle on the *entire* market you're looking at. You want to be knowledgeable about all the players in your market of choice. You also want to be aware of what interests them.

Let's say the market you've decided on is small to medium-sized private advertising and PR agencies. Is there a newspaper or magazine specific to that industry? What are their industry trade associations and who are the members? Can you become a member and get the membership directory? Who are the accountants and attorneys that specialize in working with them? Which accountants and attorneys have the biggest and best practices for this industry in your area? Which have the best reputation? Sometimes a city will provide a list of businesses, breaking them down by size, rank, and/or revenue, and even may list their major clients. Is there one for your area? If so, find it and subscribe to it. See if the local bookstore carries a Book of Lists for your city or state. If it does, buy it and use it as your bible. Find out who the PR companies are representing and what products the ad agencies are advertising. Get in front of all these people. Tell them your story, how you do business, what your strengths are, and that their business is your main focus. Make it your goal to get executives at 5 to 10 of the 50 top agencies as clients within twelve months. This is realistic and doable. Once done, you'll have an excellent base on which to drive deeper into that market.

I recently ran across a mortgage broker who has a clear vision of his market. He works for a rapidly growing, very vibrant mortgage company. I called him because I wanted his personal business. I asked him about his market and who he does business with. His response was, "I do the mortgages for the people behind the gates in this area of the state." I loved it. The term *behind the gates* was perfect. When he said that, I knew exactly what his market was and who he dealt with every day. It made me feel like I needed to work on my answer to that question.

Another Top Gun financial advisor that I interviewed for this book answered the same question with "executives and retirees." There are two markets with totally different sets of concerns, but both markets have specific needs he can identify and fill. Neither market depends on the other. In good economic periods executives do well and in poor economic periods, people are often forced into retirement. His knowledge of retirement planning comes into play during tough times, and in good times, his knowledge of stock options and investing for executives comes into play. It's a very good model and he has done well into the seven figures for many years. He has one person who makes calls for him and helps with the management of the money. They share an assistant. It's a small team operation, but a successful, profitable, and efficient one. To get new business, he mails invitations to executives, inviting them to schedule a personal consultation. The invitations are printed on high-quality stock with gold lettering. They are very simple and direct, but look fantastic. He gets responses. The response rate may not be very high, he admits, but that is offset by the quality of the prospects that do respond. They are usually both highly qualified and motivated to do business with him right away.

He has an approach to each market that works. He knows the core concerns of the retiree. They want income and safety, so that's what he brings them in a unique fashion. He knows the core concerns of the corporate executives. They want to minimize taxes and build their wealth. He brings that to them in a unique fashion. He has a strategy to reach into each market, and he executes it consistently every day.

## Creating the Pitch

On the first call you have about ten to fifteen seconds to make your introduction and say something that will hold the prospect for another ten to fifteen seconds. Lead with a concept or product that is appropriate for the current environment, such as making money in the market without risking capital. Or, you could say that you believe one of the only ways you can be assured of a positive return on your investment in this kind of market is to find lower risk yield plays. Then simply ask for the opportunity to stop by and share what you have in mind, perhaps over a cup of coffee some morning before work at his or her office, because that would be more convenient for them. Very casual, very low key and informal, nonthreatening, designed for success using behavioral psychology.

The approach is designed to find out if the prospect is willing to spend a few moments with you. If the prospect is receptive to the idea, you can ask the necessary questions to get the green lights. What size portfolio is he or she currently dealing with? Where, if at all, does he or she have other investments? If you brought something to the table that looked good, could a decision be made to invest within 30 days? How you elicit the information is truly a matter of what you're comfortable with and every one on the team will usually have his or her own way of getting to the answers. But it's important to get the green lights. Otherwise, you risk taking a lot of time and effort with unqualified prospects. We call these meetings *airballs,* and they really hurt. If someone on the team is consistently setting up airball meetings, he or she just doesn't get it, and ought to either make the necessary adjustments or move on.

The pitch you give to prospective clients should say no more than three things: Introduce yourself and your firm, explain why you're calling, and ask a question. Beyond that, you're wasting their time. Remember that your call is an unscheduled interruption of their day. Don't prolong it; get to the point. You want to meet them. If they ask, tell them why you want to meet. If they don't ask, and you've done a good job of prescreening (you know there is a high probability they are highly qualified), then just book the appointment. If they aren't receptive to a meeting, then go on to the next call. The next call will be more receptive. Sometime during a day of calls like the one described next, you will find one, two, or three people who are receptive to a meeting. And that's all you need.

Here's an example of a typical call to a successful businessperson I might have read about in the local business journal:

"Mr. Johnson, my name is Scott Kimball. I'm a Managing Director at Big Bull Securities in Atlanta and I read about you in the paper this weekend. I work with successful business owners like yourself, but I limit my practice to only 50 important relationships. I'm looking to add a few really great clients, and after reading about you, I wanted to call to see if you'd be interested in having a cup of coffee with me later in the week, perhaps before work on Thursday or Friday at your office, because that would be more convenient for you?"

"I don't know. Why do you want to meet with me, Scott?"

"Listen. You're a successful businessperson running an active, growing business. You're making money. You have a limited amount of time. If you have many of the issues my other clients are dealing with, you can benefit from my work with them. You may be interested in hearing how we're helping them reduce their taxes, prepare for their retirement, and make money in the markets without risking large capital losses. I'd just like to share with you these things and see where it takes us."

"Well, I don't know. I'm pretty busy."

"I know and I'm sensitive to that. If you have a cup of coffee in the morning, that's as long as this will take, unless you want it to go longer."

"Okay. How about Thursday at 9:00 AM?"

"Done. Thank you. I'll see you then. By the way, do you have an e-mail address? I'd like to have my assistant send you an introduction to our team and our contact information in case you need to call us."

Once you get someone to agree to a meeting time, e-mail the prospect a thank you note and an attached file that he or she can open and print. The file might contain a bio, a photo, information regarding the nature of your practice, and bios on your team and the firm. Our firm spent some money on company photos. They show us in our real working environment with plenty of technology all around. They also took shots of company headquarters and our trading floors. It makes a nice presentation. Whatever you send should be approved by your firm and make your prospective client feel good about the upcoming meeting.

In my office, we shoot for three to five meetings a week per registered individual on the team. Let's say your team consists of three registered people, but two are younger support people or callers. If you're the primary presenter, you'd be making nine to fifteen presentations per week. That's nine presentations a week for 50 weeks. If you can close one out nine, you've got 50 clients. Making nine presentations a week will make you pretty darn good at presenting, or at least it should. More importantly, with this many appointments, one meeting is not going to make or break your month or year. There's no hint of desperation.

Your pipeline of prospects is full. This allows you to fill or kill with confidence and keep the sales cycle short.

Personally, I feel better knowing that I have a lot of meetings. I can be loose and say what I really think. I am confident and upbeat, which in turn leaves my prospective client feeling confident and upbeat. If we're going to limit ourselves to 50 relationships, our clients, both prospective and established, should feel special to be included. It may sound a bit arrogant, but think about it. Let's be honest. For a long time now, the twenty-year bull market has allowed a lot of people in this business to stick around who shouldn't be there any more. People who don't know what they are doing are now getting out of the business. Many in this business don't know what they are doing. Few are providing their customers with a higher level of thinking or bringing them unique ideas to reduce risk, reduce taxes, protect their principal, and deliver enhanced returns. Most people probably do not have your level of experience, your special concern, or your knowledge of their situation. As a result, it really is to their benefit to see you, not the other way around. Thinking of your calls in this way gives you the confidence that comes through to the prospect.

## Overcoming Objections on the Call

You are going to come across *many* people who say that they don't want to hear what you have to say. They are entitled to that option, of course. However, I have wonderful clients today that started off telling me they weren't interested. Fortunately, I was able to change their minds. People expect you to be like every other salesperson who walks through the door.

You've got to convince them that you are not. Here are a few initial responses and the ways you can overcome them.

**I already have a financial advisor.** "I'm sure you do and I'm sure he's a really nice guy, but how smart is he honestly? How well has he done in this market? Is he bringing you a high level of thinking as it relates to your portfolio, your money, and your taxes? The reason I ask is that in ten minutes with me, you will absolutely know without a doubt that you are dealing with someone who is different than most of the people in this industry. If in ten minutes you don't see that, then you just give me the high sign and I'll shake your hand and leave, no harm done."

**I do all my own investing.** "Do you really like doing that? Honestly, isn't that getting a bit weird these days? The reason I ask is that these markets are becoming more and more volatile every month. Investments you would think are sound turn out to be terrible. Managing serious amounts of money is a full-time job. Five years ago, 5 percent of the volume on the stock exchange was hedge fund money. Now it can be as much as 30 or 40 percent on a given day, which explains the high volatility. The tax laws change every year, there are new vehicles you can use now to save and defer taxes, there are new vehicles that will allow you to invest in the stock market and have a guarantee that your principal is protected. My point is, if you don't do this for a living, you're going to miss out on some really good ideas you can use to make your financial life better in some critical and important way. This is what I do every day. We stay on top of it for our clients. We work with some of the most successful businesspeople in the community, and have some good ideas that have come about with recent changes in the law that you may be able to take advantage of. Let's have a cup of coffee and a few minutes together, and see where it takes us."

People who do all their own investing are often the same people who do their own taxes. These are people with a personal problem or no money, in my opinion. They believe they are smarter than almost anyone else out there, and they don't trust anyone. If you disagree, tell me why I'm wrong. Who can possibly keep up with the new tax laws? Who can possibly keep up with all the different investment choices, sector rotations, economic changes, currency's rising and falling, oil process rising and falling and what that does to the tire industry, and the price of whatever in the whatever sector? My wife came home the other day and told me she had forward purchased 500,000 CD-ROM cases—you know, the clear plastic protective cases. Why, I asked. Because the price of these things is highly sensitive to oil prices, and her company didn't want to get caught paying three times the normal price for these things due to what looked like a possible shortage of oil on the world market in the next twelve months. This could impact them, albeit only slightly, but it could impact any company that has to have these little things to protect their CDs. Software and music companies are obvious. How can one person keep up on all that kind of information? These people are usually problems, even if you can strong-arm them into giving you some of their money to invest.

I'm not interested. I don't invest my money. I have it all in mutual funds. "If you're in mutual funds, you are an investor, sir," I said. He explained that he meant he wasn't a big-time stock trader or anything. I told him that I felt I could help him, and that at the very least, I could probably give him a good idea or two and that I could probably get a good idea from him on something he knows about as well. I suggested we get together and he agreed, reluctantly. Turned out he had $3 million in the "noninvestment mutual fund investments." On top of that, he was selling his business and would pick up another couple of million. We hit it off.

I had another fellow tell me he wasn't interested because he felt all of us Wall Street types were criminals, used car salesmen, and couldn't be trusted. I told him that I certainly could understand why he would think that, what with all the recent press involving shady stock deals. But I assured him that I was a third-generation Eagle Scout, a graduate from UCLA, an officer in my fraternity, a happily married man of eleven years with three wonderful children, a member of ten national associations in economics and finance, a former professional baseball player, a patron of several charities, including the Boys Club and the Boy Scouts, as well as a regular volunteer in the community.

He was silent. So I then said, "As you can see, I'm actually an all right guy, and I guarantee that in ten minutes you'll be able to see that I'm different from just about everyone you've ever met in my business. So, what do you say, let's get together for a cup of coffee and see where it takes us?" He actually apologized for saying what he said, and he said he'd be happy to get together.

## Getting through the Screener

The screener is the person, usually a female executive assistant, who answers the phone for the big prospect (BP) you're trying to reach. It is this person's job to make sure you do not bother BP. BP has told her that if she lets anyone through with investment calls, she's going to catch hell. She has already caught hell a number of times for this, so she is very diligent. If the prospect you are calling is a high-profile professional, or the CEO of a high-profile company, you will encounter the Top Gun screeners. I love it when I encounter them. They are truly the best in the business. The way they block you, twist you up, make you feel like a little bug, and get you to cough up the fact that you don't know Mr. Big—all the while being pleasant, firm, and professional—well, it is a beautiful thing. When you encounter one of these pros, you just have to smile as you hang up defeated. You didn't even get close to getting through. She beat you, man. She is the best of the best. She did her job. And you have to respect that.

So here are three solutions.

**1. Enroll her in your cause, deferring to her power and expertise.** You have to understand that she is, at that very moment, the most important person in the world to you. Why? Because she has control of who gets through and who does not. Show her the respect she's due! Be honest with her right up front. Ask her to help you. She is in this position because she is fiercely loyal and has an innate desire and ability to help people. If you try to blow by her, you'll offend her and she'll block you. Your only chance is to enroll her in your cause, letting her know that you respect her power.

The toughest screeners often know who you are and what you're trying to accomplish just by the tone in your voice. They are better than you because they field about 100 of these calls every day. There is no way you can beat her in most cases. So don't try. Enroll her in your cause and defer to her power and expertise.

Here's a typical call with a Top Gun screener.

Screener: "Hello, BP's office. May I help you?"

TOP GUN: "Well, I hope so. This is Scott Kimball. I'm a Managing Director at Big Bull Securities. Is BP in today?"

Screener: "I'm sorry Mr. Kimball, but BP is very busy today. Does he know you?"

TOP GUN: "Possibly. We've run into each other a few times I believe and have some mutual friends." (Shift gears/shift tone of voice.) "Listen, I need your help here. My company has a very short list of leading businessmen and women in Atlanta who we believe we should meet. BP is right there on top of the list. I have been told that it is my job to get a meeting with BP. Can you help me here? What should I do in order to get a few minutes over a cup of coffee some morning? Does BP like that sort of thing, or do you have another idea about how we can arrange a meeting? You tell me how to do it."

In a few sentences, I deferred to her—and admitted it. I showed her that I know she's the one with the power here. I appealed to her natural sense of wanting to help people, and I enrolled her in my cause by using the word *we*. I brought her over onto my team, which is exactly where I want her to be.

At this point, if you find yourself in a similar position, you've got to take her lead. If she tells you that you're out of luck, you probably are. If she tells you that she'll talk to him and get back to you, she probably will. Sometimes she'll put you on hold and check with him. And every once in a while, she'll get BP on the phone right then and there.

**2. The authoritarian approach.**  Be an actor. Use your voice as a tool. Your voice is the only instrument you have when you're trying to get through to someone over the phone. Use it like a singer uses his or her voice, like an instrument. Inflection, tone, tenor, pitch, volume, pace, and tempo—all these are nuances in a call that can either help or hurt your chances of getting through. If you sound like a salesperson, I guarantee you'll never get past the screener. But if you sound sincere and spontaneous, you've got a shot. It's a good idea to record your voice. Record your colleagues' voices, too, and play them back. Critique each other and try different ways of presenting your pitches. I think I have a voice that sounds like I'm a 50-year-old executive. It can be very commanding and powerful sounding in its tone or, I'm told, my voice can be soothing and pleasant to the ear.

I have used this approach occasionally and I've had some success. I act a bit the confused and busy executive who is returning calls as fast as he can. Using the tenor of my voice and sounding very distracted, I say, "Yes, hello, this is Scott Kimball. Is Ed there?"

Sometimes it helps to shuffle papers on the desk for background affect or actually talk to other people at the same time, as if there is a lot going on in your office. No doubt, she will ask, "What is this regarding, sir?"

With all the confusion supposedly going on around me, I simply pretend I didn't catch it. "I'm sorry, I didn't get that. It's a crazy morning here. Is he there? I'm supposed to speak with Ed Johnson today. Is he there?"

She'll probably try again, "What is this regarding, sir?"

I only answer with who I am again, not what this is regarding. "This is Scott Kimball. I'm a Managing Director at Big Bull." Immediately, I pull the phone away from my mouth, keeping the earpiece to my ear, but start telling an imaginary someone in my office to do something. "Right, Joey, just do the reallocation the way we discussed and buy 10,000 at the market in the morning. Be careful of the volume and wait until about 10:00 AM."

By now, I'm hoping she's got the idea that I'm a busy man and don't have time to waste repeating myself, that she'll give up, and put me through. After all, I'm driving *her* nuts and she's got some important things to do before the day ends, too. Sometimes it works and sometimes it doesn't. She is just as likely to slam-dunk me for being a jerk, so if you ever try this, do so at your own risk. The important thing is to have fun, but be professional. It's a game; it's not personal. If she slam-dunks you, it's not personal. If the prospect won't get on the line, that's not personal either. Usually it's just timing. Sometimes you just hit people at the wrong time. It's possible to call back the very next day and find the tone of the call to be completely different.

3. The familiarity ploy. Occasionally, I use the ruse of familiarity with the prospect to get through the executive secretary. It's not particularly innovative, but it's been known to work from time to time. This is where you use familiar names (both yours and the prospect's) to imply that the two of you are already good friends. "Yes, hello, this is Dutch. Is Eddie in?"

She'll buzz into his office and tell him there's a "Dutch" on the line asking for "Eddie." Often, the prospect will get on the phone. First, because its fun to talk to guys named Dutch, and second, he may think he knows you or ran into you at some event or golf course because you asked for him by a nick-name. William is "Bill," Richard is "Dick," Robert is "Bob,"—you get the idea. It doesn't always work, but it works a lot!

## Prefiltering

Once you've gathered the names of everyone that looks like they are of substance and potentially influential within that market, you have to reach them through one of the methods we've discussed. Calling out of a phone directory is the least productive method of prospecting, because you haven't done any prefiltering. You don't know whom you're talking to. You add to your productivity by increasing the odds of having a successful call if you prefilter.

If you are a financial planner or advisor to individuals, and looking to build your business, you have to look for the people who are making good money. You want clients who are expanding their businesses, buying more space, adding production capacity, and hiring people when everyone else is laying them off. Search the newspaper for articles about franchises that are expanding. Look for companies that are relocating into your area and may be moving a large number of people with them. Sometimes new arrivals spend much less on their new home than they had on their former one. It has to do with land values from state to state. But that price difference can reach into the hundreds of thousands. People need to find a place for that surplus income.

Then there are always those current residents who want to trade up. People who are buying or building new houses generally don't do that when things are tough for them, right? Why not go to the new clubs that are being built in your area and find out who is buying the homes on the golf course? Get to know the builders there. Why not make them your clients, and then a referral source of people moving into the area? Get them to refer the names of the new homebuyers to you *before* they hit the newspaper, because after that it is officially public record.

In bad markets you want to find the individuals, businesses, or companies that make big money during these tough times. There are always people who own businesses that run counter to the economic cycle. Bankruptcy attorneys are an excellent, yet obvious, example. They're feeling good, they're flush with money, they are socking it away, and they are psychologically in the right place for you to approach them. There are others in that category. Generally speaking, doctors, health care professionals, hospital executives, waste management/trash/disposal/recycling business owners, and divorce or family law attorneys do well in spite of the market.

Another form of prefiltering is simply being more intelligent about who you call. If prospecting is a filtering process, aimed at finding people who are truly interested in speaking with you, then you want to spend your time optimally. Instead of cold calling names out of the phone directory, you want to be looking for the individuals and companies who might naturally have an interest in the products or services offered by your firm.

Let's assume for the moment that your company is the absolute leader in the country for separately managed account business. There is just no one out there with better solutions for the investor in this area. You are competitive in price, have the best statements and analysis, and the best managers as well as overall performance. This is a large business for the firm, so you can pretty much rest assured that it's not going to be pushed aside for something new anytime soon.

If you select this as one of the business lines you will represent to the public, then part of your prefiltering process has to include looking for people or institutions that have a natural interest in this kind of management. We're talking about people who have a large amount of money to invest, a fairly decent level of sophistication about the investment business, a rational expectation of what performance means, and a decent appreciation for diversification between asset classes, managers, and investment styles. Who are these people? Where do you find them? That's up to you to determine. I've provided you with lots of ideas. *You* have to do the work in finding out who, within your community, fits the profile, who has a natural need, desire, and understanding of this particular product and service. People who will work well with you. Perhaps you should consider networking through accountants who have clients who fit the profile but are not happy with their current advisor. Better yet, position yourself as the person who takes over accounts when the smaller client grows up, sells his or her business, and outgrows his or her current advisor.

Maybe your firm also has a strong derivatives desk. Virtually no one can beat you in this area. Why wouldn't you look to call groups of people or institutions that have a true need for a strong derivatives desk and tell them you want to cover them for the firm? Be honest about wanting a shot at their derivatives business and ask if they'll permit you to bid on it when it comes up. This is potentially an entirely different group of clients with an entirely different profile, which is good for the diversification of your business.

## Filtering

Prefiltering is about finding people with whom you may want to do business. Filtering is about finding the people who want to do business with you. Too many of us in this line of work appear to be desperate. We're walking around with the proverbial cup in our hand, practically begging for an appointment with someone, believing that if we just had a shot at spending a few minutes talking with him or her, we could win the business.

As I've said before, we're not here to change people's religions. We're not pioneers. That type of work is too hard and has a low success ratio. It is difficult to change someone's mind if that mind is not open to change. People will change if and when they believe a change would be beneficial. If there's no need or no "pain" as we discussed earlier, it is unlikely that a change is imminent. In such cases, you have to do something hard that old-time aluminum-siding type salesmen were famous for. They called it "creating the need." What they would do is choose one house on the block and give the owners a heck of a deal on having the house done in their new siding. Then they would take pictures of it and walk up and down through the neighborhood with a camera on a tripod, pretending to take pictures of the houses where the siding had yet to be put up. The people in the houses would come out, of course, and ask what was going on. One of the salesmen would explain that they were doing a series of before and after photos, and that they needed a "before" house picture. They already had the after photo—the house down the street with the beautiful siding already in place. Would it be an inconvenience to use *this* house for the before photo? Of course, it was not going to be okay with that homeowner. Who would want to be identified with *any* before picture?

Now the salesperson had an easy segue into his pitch. Perhaps this homeowner, too, would be interested in learning about the advantages to aluminum siding! The technique may have been a bit cheesy, but it was effective. These guys took people who were perfectly content with the appearance of their house and created a need for aluminum siding within a few minutes.

Effective or not, this is tough work. Too tough, in my opinion. Wouldn't it be easier to simply go looking for people who have already made up their minds that their houses needed a new look? Those people have already done half of your work for you. Now all you have to do is show them that you have the best and most logical solution to their problem.

Specific to our business, we want to find people who know or strongly suspect that they need a change in money management. In fact, we want them to be uncomfortable in their current situation, so much so that they are actually looking for that new relationship in an active manner. If you have 100 conversations with new people in a week, you're only looking for those five to ten that have already done most of the work for you. They have recognized a flaw in the way their money is being managed now or have heard about something new that they'd like to try. Those are the clients you want.

It's like when we were kids and we would look around the rocks on the shore for crabs. We would look in all the crevices and under all the rocks along the beach. We'd turn over hundreds of rocks in a day. We weren't trying to convince some rock that it should have a crab under it. We were just looking for the rock that already had the crab under it. Pretty soon, we learned that certain size rocks in certain positions had a high probability of housing a crab, so we went to those rocks first. Why did we do that? Because even then we were good prospectors. We were looking for a way to cut down on unnecessary work by lifting up rocks that were highly likely to have the crab underneath them, and thus, increasing our hit ratio.

## Qualifying (Getting the Green Lights)

Once you've found someone who has done most of the work for you and is interested in seeing you, it's time to qualify. Every person has to make up his or her own mind as to what qualifying questions they'll ask and how much their minimum might be. For certain products or services the number will differ significantly. A $10 million cash management account is small. A $10 million individual investment account is large. You have to decide what the number is based upon the service you are offering or talking about.

In general, you'll be looking for someone who has the money that you can work with effectively, depending upon the product or service areas in which you have chosen to specialize.

In the area of cash management for example, you'll need to ask a qualifying question such as, "How much money are you currently managing in your cash management program?" If the answer is less than $10 million, this is probably not a company or institution you can help. If you're talking to an individual, and you ask, "About how much do you have invested in the markets now, including stocks, bonds, and cash combined?" and he or she comes back with a number like $1 million, this may be someone you want to get to know. The next question is then a further filter. "Really, that's quite a nice sum. Congratulations for making that happen. Listen, a number of people we've been talking to are making some changes right now to take advantage of some important shifts in the market. Are you entirely happy with the way your funds are being handled now, or would you be interested in hearing some solid thinking as it pertains to your money and the current environment?" If the answer is positive, you've got a qualified appointment.

We call this "getting the green lights." Positive answers to the filtering and qualifying questions make for green lights.

- Is this person interested at all?

- Does this person have enough money to matter?

- Is this person willing to meet you soon—within 30 days?

- Is this person the decision maker, or will there be others involved?

Before we go on, I want to reemphasize something I said earlier: *Everyone* who wants it is entitled to financial advice and money management. The issue is not whether prospects have enough money to matter to you or me, but whether they have enough money to truly utilize the firepower of the firm and the sophistication level of what we do. For example, some types of money management literally dictate that in order to effectively reach the level of diversification and cost structure necessary to make it viable for the client, the client has to have at least $1 million.

Just because we aren't the right money managers for someone doesn't mean that his or her money isn't worthy of thought and care. The fact that a person *wants* to protect and strengthen his or her assets is commendable. And as flip as I've been about who is and isn't worthy of our attention, you have to understand I am trying to make a point about the value of your time as it compares to your personal goals. But, there is a financial advisor out there for virtually everyone and anyone who wants one.

# CHAPTER SIX

# COLD CALLING— STILL NUMBER ONE

*The obstacle is the path.*

BUDDHA

If you don't get anything else out of this book, get this: People who are truly interested in doing business don't do it with people they don't know. And people don't really feel like they know you until they've met you. As a result, you must go face to face, one on one, one by one, in order to get to the serious business of discussing the critical core concerns of the prospect, and position yourself properly in his or her mind so that when the prospect becomes a client, you can do the business you want to do the way you want to do it.

So the first thing to do when cold calling is to ask for the appointment. This sets prospects off balance. They are not used to this. Everyone else is calling and pitching them something. By asking for the appointment first, you accomplish two things at once: First, you imply that you already know they are qualified because you do your homework before you call. Second, you're different. You haven't pitched them anything, you haven't asked them for any personal information, you're simply asking for ten minutes of their time. You're serious. You're not trying to sell them something over the phone. Your purpose for calling isn't to sell them something; it's to see if they will meet with you. The prospect usually then asks *you* a question like "Who are you?" or "Why would we get together?" Well, thanks for asking! Tell them why you want to meet them.

You don't have to give them a reason why you're calling—you already told them why: to book an appointment. Now you can get down to business.

If they ask, offer a valid reason for getting together. Psychologically, you will have taken them from having a phone conversation with you to imagining what it is you'll be discussing when you meet. You have transported them, in their mind, to an appointment with you at their office. "I just wanted to hear about what you're doing primarily, but I can also share with you what we're doing for some of our best clients who have similar concerns, if you're interested."

If they will not meet you, shred the card and *move on.* If they won't meet you, for whatever reason, they won't do business with you. Either they have no money and aren't willing to tell you, or there is some other probable deal killer in the mix. This rule is absolutely 99 percent infallible. If they will not meet with you, they will not do business with you. If your shredder is going strong every day, then you'll know you're working and accomplishing something.

Another thing to remember is to verify your assumptions about the qualifications of prospects only if necessary. If you know potential clients are qualified, then don't waste their time or yours. If they have been referred to you, and they agree to a meeting, you shouldn't qualify them on the call. Remember, you're trying to select people from various sources in your target market that you have a high level of confidence are qualified. This means that nine of every ten will probably qualify, but, if necessary, you have to ask the question on the call. It's perfectly valid to ask. You don't want to waste their time, but it's not purely selfish. "What are you doing currently that's working for you?" or "Do you currently have any investments you're happy with? Really? What are they?" Open-ended, softly probing questions that may elicit some insight into the financial picture of the prospect are the goal.

The key, however, is to ask the qualifying question last— after the prospect has agreed to the meeting. There are reasons for this. First, that the prospect has already agreed to meet you is a commitment they have already made you. They are more likely to be honest with you at that point than earlier in the call. Second, if they haven't agreed to meet with you yet, what do you really care whether they are qualified? Their qualification only matters to you if you will see them, right?

Everyone on your team needs to do his or her pushups. Someone on the team, including you, should be making cold calls. If it's just you, then fine. If you can get another person on the team to call for you, then even better. But you have to call with them so they learn and stay motivated. In general, a good cold caller should be able to book three to five qualified appointments for you every week. If you can generate another three to five per week, and you can get another one or two from other sources, you're seeing seven to twelve new people every week. Out of that seven to twelve, perhaps only one eventually becomes a client. That's 50. One year of seeing seven to twelve new people every week means you'll have met with 400 or 500 people. Remember, you *don't* want all of them to become clients. Not all of them will be right for you, and you won't be right for all of them. You're just looking for that one every week who is the right client, who can utilize the firepower of the firm.

## The Basic Rules of Cold Calling

- *Have a script.* Unless you're really good, you must have a script. Even great salespeople write out a script, outline, or guide, and rehearse it out loud with their teammates so that it sounds good. Putting the words together in a manner that is concise, logical, and effective is the goal. You have to know where you want the conversation to go and keep it on track towards its conclusion.

- *Start.* Don't worry too much about how perfect the script is; let the world shape your script. You'll hear the things you say that cause the prospects to listen harder, the phrases that make them respond positively. Gradually refine the script so that it is very smooth and very clean, so it has a high impact, but is concise and yields the precise information you need.

- *Sound natural.* There is nothing worse than making a call and sounding like a salesperson reading from a script. Use a tape recorder. Tape ten calls a week. Pop the tape into your car and listen to it when you have a long drive or listen to it with your partner or senior broker or assistant at the end of a day. Laugh at how bad you sounded on some of them. You have to have a sense of humor about this. You have to be able to laugh at yourself. But listen and remember and replay the really good ones, where you were successful in booking the appointment and said some good stuff that got you there. Write it down. Rehearse saying it exactly like that call.

- *Get the green lights.* The call should determine if the person is interested and is qualified financially to do business with you. Don't try to mask it—they know why you're calling. They know that you need to know whether they have any money and whether they are willing to let you invest it if they like what you have to say, meet them face to face, and work for a reputable firm. So ask the questions. Find out if they have the money, they are willing to invest, and they are willing to act in the *next few days.* If they will have a cup of coffee with you to discuss the opportunity in the next few days or weeks, perhaps on their way to work, or at the office early one morning, then they qualify. If they tell you to call back in six months, they are not qualified. Remember, you're after the ripe fruit— you're not planting young seedlings that you hope grow up to have fruit, you need to go to the orchards where the trees have grown for many years and the fruit is ripe.

- *Be courteous and professional.* Even though you may use humor or some other way of staying loose, and you should develop a comfortable style of your own, be professional and courteous. It's okay to have a sense of humor, but not to be crude, flippant, or disrespectful. Remember that you are talking to people about their money. They like to see you have a personality, but they aren't going to hire you because you are the funniest broker in town. Self-deprecating humor can be endearing and shows humility, and people like people who are humble.

- *Fill or kill often.* The *fill or kill* is a type of order used on Wall Street. When you put this on your ticket, it's telling the trader to either fill the entire order or kill the entire order, but don't go half way or execute a partial on this order. The abbreviation is FOK. When you've called on prospects, perhaps you've talked to them a few times and tried to get appointments, then called back because you were encouraged for some reason. At some point, you have to decide before the call that either the prospect is going to meet with you or you're shredding the card. This brings up a good point. You should spend a few hundred dollars for a good shredder machine. First, your work, even your notes, is often about clients' private financial business, and it is your job to keep that confidential. Second, however, when you are calling or filling and killing, and you run across someone who should be forever forgotten, the shredder is a fun place to put them. It feels good. In fact, it is our goal to put a lot of prospects in the shredder every week, particularly on fill or kill days. I can't emphasize how important this is. Keeping names and numbers and cards and lists of prospects hanging around and hanging around is the fastest way to fool yourself into thinking you have something going on. *You don't.* You just have a big mess of people who don't want to talk to you, who are leading you on or wasting your time. Call them, if they won't meet with you, they aren't going to do business with you. Shred 'em and move on.

Your prospect cannot see you. He or she cannot see that you work in a nice office, dress nicely, have powerful computers, and are a legitimate caller and a solid community citizen. People who are scumbags use this fact to their advantage, but for you, it works to your disadvantage, because you want them to know that you are legitimate, that you are a solid citizen and a professional. So, you have to work hard on how you come across on the phone. You have to build the correct image with only partial use of the human sensory system. You only have your voice and the words you say.

Your voice is an instrument. It can subtly communicate so much simply with its volume, inflection, tone, accent, cadence, and pace. Actors and singers learn how to use their voice to deliver their lines so that they fit the situation, so that they have the proper impact on the audience. You can do this, too.

For example, when someone you've called fires back at your opening line with a stern, "Why the heck would I want to get together with you?" you can come back with your reply in a tone softer than the one you led with, but with words that have high impact. "Mr. Johnson, I only call on the people I've carefully selected as someone I want to do business with. I don't call out of a telephone book. I know exactly who you are. You're a player in your industry. I only deal with the players. I want to come and have a cup of coffee with you in the morning, Okay?" Be disarming. Use your voice as an instrument. Be an actor. Play with it. Vary your tone and observe what gets the best response.

## Conclusion

Cold calling is still the number one way to efficiently determine if the prospect is worth spending more time face to face with. You're not trying to convince people who don't want to see you to meet with you, you're just trying to find those people who are naturally interested in seeing you, who are open to a meeting, who have already determined on their own that they should be looking to another advisor with a better way of doing things.

By approaching your cold calling efforts in this manner, with this frame of mind, rejection is not at all stressful. It becomes your friend. You begin to look forward to it, and without it each day, you will feel uncomfortable. You will have turned what is normally uncomfortable to most people into something that is comfortable for you. The beauty of this is that doing this thing that has become comfortable for you, but is still uncomfortable to most, will make you a success. People making cold calls, or developing a new business, must feel rejection every day or they are not doing their job.

# CHAPTER SEVEN

# TECHNOLOGY AND PROSPECTING

## Bloomberg

I've mentioned Bloomberg several times in this book because it's quite honestly an amazing machine. It is a computer terminal used by financial professionals all over the world. The Bloomberg database is vast and its analytics in virtually every area of finance are robust. The capabilities of the machine are so far reaching that it is a good idea to simply realize up front that you will never in your lifetime understand all of its functionality. Using the machine takes some getting used to because it has a customized keyboard that is different than anything most people have ever seen. The first time I looked at it, it made no sense to me whatsoever. After working with it for a few days, taking what seemed to be tiny baby steps of discovery, I found myself saying out loud, "This is *cool!*" If you haven't used it yet, I'm sure you'll do the same thing. And then you'll wonder why you weren't told about this Bloomberg thing a long time ago.

One use of Bloomberg that is often overlooked is its ability to assist you tremendously in your prospecting efforts. For example, it ranks shareholders by position size for virtually every public company. If you are looking to target a particular industry, it can search that industry by SIC code and pull up all the public companies for you. Furthermore, it can pull them up for just a state, a region, or any other way you want it broken down. It can print you a report, stating the name of the company ranked by size, followed by the name of the CFO, and then the phone number. If you want to add total revenue, it will. If the amount of cash on hand at the company is important to you, it will list that. It will give you shareholder information and contact names and numbers.

This machine can provide you with virtually any specific fact you want to know relating to financial services. If you only want to see software companies that have more than $100 million market capitalization, are profitable, and have more than $10 million in cash on the balance sheet, it will give you that information. If you notice a company stock has gone up dramatically in the past six months, perhaps some of the executives or large shareholders would be interested in selling some of that stock. By typing in the company stock symbol and stroking a few keys, you can get a list of the executives, their phone numbers, their titles, and their stock holdings in the company. You'll know where they went to college, how old they are, where they worked before, how many kids they have, and how much they made in the past few years or more. Many have pictures of the executive on the screen. For the shareholders, you simply click on the name of the entity that is listed as a shareholder and it takes you to another screen that provides you with the contact name and phone number for that shareholder. This allows you to call the contact person and feel them out about their position on the stock and whether there is any interest in selling or hedging.

Bloomberg provides a daily listing of mergers and acquisitions worldwide. Again, this can be broken down to any region you desire. The same thing applies to SEC filings, changes in ownership filings, insider intent to sell filings SIC codes—just about everything you can find on EDGAR (the SEC database) is there. Once you've screened for the particular filing you want in the region you want, all you have to do is click and it pops up on your screen. You can either read the filing or print it out for reading later.

Bloomberg's capabilities go so much farther than this that it's almost a disservice to talk about it strictly in terms of prospecting. In fact, its usefulness as a prospecting tool is almost an accidental afterthought of the system. Originally it was devised to bring hard-to-find information about the bond market to bond traders. It has evolved from there into something quite remarkable. Of course, Bloomberg isn't cheap. It runs about $1,500 per month, but in certain areas of the investment business, it is essential. Once you get used to the machine and learn how to use it (which can take a few months), it will be something you'd kill for before letting it go. If it lands you one or two significant clients or transactions a year, it pays for itself. Then all the analytics and other capabilities it gives you that help you do your job better are free.

## Internet

We already discussed the concept of going after money in motion. Company insiders who are selling stock have to file with the SEC when they sell or plan to sell stock. Mergers and acquisitions are another time in which company insiders and large shareholders are seeing their assets turned into cash or another stock. The sites that can be helpful in these areas are <www.thompsonfn.com>, <www.mergernetwork.com>, <www.corporateaffiliations.com>, <www.freeedgar.com>, <www.corporateinformation.com>, and <www.tenkwizard .com>. Other directories with information on thousands of companies, both public and private, are <www.realtimietrad ers.com>, <www.theonlineinvestor.com>, <www.hoovers .com>, and <www.yahoo.finance.com>. Often, when you have found an interesting story on someone and there is no information easily available in any of the above sites, you can search the net using <www.google.com>, <www.infousa.com>, or <www .whitepages.com>.

I recently attended a seminar given by Kip Gregory, who is coming out with a book of his own soon. Kip is the master of using the Internet as a tool in prospecting campaigns and efforts. One of the most enlightening things I learned was that you can type a letter into a Word document, get it approved by your compliance department, then download the letter to the U.S. Post Office on their Web site, and specify where you want it to go by ZIP code and other factors, and sure enough, they do all the fulfillment for you. You never leave your office, you never sort and stamp and stuff. If a mailing campaign is part of what you do, you should go to <www.usps.gov> and check out their capabilities.

If you haven't found out already, you will learn soon that a good research assistant is invaluable. He or she can make your life infinitely easier by helping you to be better prepared and well informed. There are just not enough hours in a week to make all your calls, see all your appointments, and do all your own research. When you're in sync with your researcher, the two of you can work like a well-oiled machine. While you're calling, your research assistant can be searching the Internet for prospects that fit your profiles. He or she will know precisely the information you're looking for, and if you're really lucky, make you look like a star.

## Contact Management Software

ACT! ($199.00). From the time I opened the box, I was excited. I was up and running right away, inputting contacts into the ACT! software database within about four or five minutes. The functionality is robust and the format is customizable. ACT! is owned by a larger software company, so it has the support to be around for a while.

Although I don't write many letters, for the ones that I do write, ACT! made the process easy. While on a contact, I just click on "write letter" and the letter comes up fully formatted with my information. I only have to write the body, then print. The scheduling function is easier to operate and is presented in a cleaner, clearer manner than Outlook currently has in its design.

I like the feature that allows you to track conversations and comments you made with clients and/or prospects, as well the comments made by them. In our business this is particularly important because people sometimes tend to have selective memories about what was said in meetings. They can "forget" what you told them to do and what recommendations you suggested they take. Having a record of what each of you said is simply a mark of a good professional, even with perfect clients.

Furthermore, I like the interoperability with Microsoft Outlook. The last thing I wanted to do was devote hundreds of hours to the task of manually entering my Outlook names into ACT!. I didn't have to. It synchronized my data with Outlook easily and, because my assistant drops new contact information into Outlook each day, it has an automatic feature that will download the information from Outlook to ACT! and vice versa.

I also like its ability to mine the database for contacts I haven't been in touch with for 30 days. This way I can make sure I contact them. Birthday reminders and other important events are also schedulable and automatic.

Many people who think they have decent contact management software try ACT! and realize that what they have is prehistoric. In my mind, it is the best contact management software for the money.

(In the interest of full disclosure, I have to state that while writing this book, I discovered that someone in my family is an officer at the company that now owns ACT!)

**GoldMine ($199.95).** GoldMine has been around a long time and it has been used by many in the financial services world because it provides a template designed specifically for the financial services professional. Like ACT! it has a number of useful features similar to those listed above with ACT!

**Microsoft.** Microsoft Outlook is not a database offering, but it can be used like one for basic database features. It really is just a front-end interface to the e-mail function. Microsoft does have Access, which is the competitive offering to the software listed above, but it costs $339 on a stand-alone basis. For $579, you can buy Microsoft XP Professional, which features a full suite of Microsoft software, including Access. If your company provides you with Microsoft Outlook and you want a Microsoft product to go with it, Access is one alternative. However, at 70 percent higher pricing for the stand-alone version, it is not a compelling offering in my opinion. Perhaps they will take advantage of Outlook being so ubiquitous and roll out an upgrade that will allow us to simply use Outlook as an alternative to buying some other vendor's software, but who knows? Until then, however, Outlook is useful for basic functions such as calendars and contact files, but intentionally lacks the features, look, and feel that is so rich in other software.

## Cell Phones

Many, if not all, of us drive to and from work each day. If this takes 45 minutes each way, that's one and a half hours that used to be down time. What are you doing with this time each day? Are you talking to your friends and planning the evening? Are you calling your clients? Reaching out and making cold calls? One of my favorite prospecting techniques is to get on the highway and look for trucks that have a business name and phone number on them. There it is, the name of the company, what they do, and their phone number and locations. The only thing missing is the name of the owner! Call the company. Ask for the owner and say it's regarding one of their trucks on Highway 12. Trust me, he or she will get on the phone. When the owner gets on, tell the truth: You're calling because your best clients are business owners who are highly successful. You were on your way home, saw the truck, and thought that the owner of the company was someone that you wanted to meet. Go into one of your pitches. Ask Mr. Owner if he has any money sitting around earning less than ___%? If the answer is yes, then say, "That's why I'm calling. If you can make ___% and have the income guaranteed by the U.S. government, pay no federal tax on that income, and have the principal guaranteed as well, does that sound like a good reason for you have a cup of coffee with me on the way into work tomorrow?"

You can make ten of these calls each way. Use a call list if you have one and can read it without endangering yourself or others. There are twenty pushups and you're not even at your desk. You can set two or three appointments while you're in the car on the way home and another one on the way into the office. You do this and I pity the financial advisor who tries to keep up with you.

## E-mail

E-mail can be a very good way to noninvasively probe and successfully reach a prospect who otherwise is unreachable. For example, I was trying to reach a very wealthy and successful restaurant chain owner, who was on the road constantly. He was never at his office, and I couldn't get his cell phone number. But he had e-mail so I sent him a message. He got back to me within 24 hours. For some people, e-mail is a preferred way to communicate, and executives have been trained to return e-mails but ignore calls from people they don't know. It's just a habit that you can take advantage of in order to make contact.

Often, if you look at a company's Web page there will be a "contact us" icon. Click on that and you may see the e-mail address format that the company uses. Even if the person you are trying to reach isn't listed there, you can mirror the format you see in the other addresses and use that for the person you are trying to reach. Type in two or three versions that you think may be close on the address line of your e-mail, and you'll be surprised how often one of them is correct. The others will bounce back to you as undeliverable.

One of the best in the business at using e-mail to reach out and make contact is a fellow named Bruce Faurot, an advisor at Janney Montgomery Scott. I've been privileged to see Bruce work with clients for a number of years, and I've seen how he has used e-mail to find business. Using Bloomberg, Bruce once noticed that there was a large block of stock in a U.S. company being held by a European investment company. Instead of calling, Bruce found their Web site and contact information.

Through a few e-mails, he was able to make contact with the partner that covered that investment. He then began an intelligent dialogue though e-mail about the position and the factors that surround its potential value, and then he asked for the business. He asked them to ship him the certificate and let him handle the disposition of the stock for them. They did. He handled the trades masterfully and wired them the money. Bruce has now positioned himself as their U.S. equity contact.

When "pinging" select individuals this way, you have to be very delicate and light in your approach. You should be very courteous and professional and direct. Remember, all you want is a meeting. No matter what they send back to you, even if it is a very nasty "get lost," you thank them. Don't forget, e-mails are permanent. You don't want to give anyone out there a reason to call the chairman of your company and forward an e-mail that makes you look bad. Be a professional.

J.W. is another master of using e-mail as a prospecting tool. J.W. uses the e-mail he receives from his clients, who copy him on jokes, and pings other people on his clients' e-mail list! Of course, he asks permission, but this is easy! He ends up getting most of his referrals this way.

E-mail is a double-edged sword. You must be very careful in your use of e-mail in general. Most of us have not been given adequate instruction in the proper use and etiquette of e-mail. From someone in the technology world who has been using e-mail for a decade or so longer than you and I, I have received some basic instruction.

First, let me repeat that e-mail is permanent. An attorney recently told me that 60 to 70 percent of his cases involve e-mail traffic in which the sender never expected anyone except the recipient to see the e-mail. In most of these cases, the information in the e-mail can be characterized as an agreement or even a contract, rather than a friendly note. Anything you write down in e-mail is a record that will be there forever. Therefore, no matter how upset you are, no matter how you've been wronged, do *not* fire off any angry e-mail response. A good adage is to write very, very little in response to questions you may be asked by clients or others. If you feel you must immediately respond by e-mail, simply say, "I'm going to call you to address this as soon as I can." Then do whatever homework you need to do and call. *There is no law that says you have to respond to an e-mail by e-mail. There is no law that says you have to respond to an e-mail immediately.* Read the e-mail, think about whether it needs to be addressed immediately, then decide how to handle it. Sometimes the best course of action is to respond to it with a phone call.

Second, because e-mail is permanent, anything you say about an investment product, program, or idea can potentially be used against you in a dispute or court case. I recently saw an e-mail from a financial advisor in which he stated to a potential investor that the attached investment was "one bad-ass awesome investment." Now, just imagine if that prospect became a client, the investment went upside down, and the client decided to show the attorney that e-mail? How will it look in front of an arbitration panel when they pull out the e-mail and ask about this statement?

Third, e-mail is very often misinterpreted. You may be in a wonderful mood while writing an e-mail to a client, and you say something that inadvertently offends him or her or is taken the wrong way. The client's reaction confuses you. How could someone think you meant that when you really meant something entirely different? A person reading an e-mail cannot see your facial expression, your mood, or your body language. He or she cannot hear the inflection in your voice. The subtleties of human communication are many, and they are stripped out of the process with e-mail. Carefully word your e-mail and be clear. Read and reread before you send. Avoid the natural desire to try to show your sharp wit or be humorous. It may just come across as flip, arrogant, or worse. Finally, don't use capital letters unless you intend to let the recipient know that you are yelling, because that is what it means to use them.

# CHAPTER EIGHT

# THE TOP GUN PROSPECTING MACHINE

The Top Gun prospecting machine is a combination of highly effective methods of bringing qualified prospective clients to you. It can be any combination of the following, as long as it (1) consists of three or more of them, (2) is comfortable for you, (3) is low cost, and (4) is done consistently.

- Cold calling

- Seminars

- Model City

- Invitations

- E-mail

- Social encounters

- Radio show or advertising

- Newspaper advertising

- Referrals from clients

- Referrals from advisors

Before we get ahead of ourselves, let's take a step back and get our heads on straight before we look at these methods.

The bottom line in our business is this: If you don't hit your numbers in sales, you're gone. It's that simple and straightforward. That's the stark reality of what we do. It's also the beauty of what we do. Think about it. There is no color barrier, gender bias, or age discrimination to the numbers. The numbers don't care and they don't lie. They are what they are. Either they are there or they are not. I think this is beautiful because there's no bullshit. It's not about who you know in the company or who your father or mother might be. It's just about doing the business. This takes all the excuses away. "I'm the wrong color, I'm a woman, I'm too short, I'm too tall, I'm too fat, I'm too skinny, I'm bald, I'm too old, I'm too young, I'm not from here, I went to the wrong college, I don't have my MBA or JD or CPA." All of the excuses for not going out and doing something to make your life a success are gone now. This is it.

In this business, there are extremely successful people who are blind and crippled. There are people who are deaf. Imagine that, a deaf person in a business in which you are supposed to listen to a customer and communicate and persuade! They exist. I know them. I've met them. They produce. There are people in this business who have had to overcome a lot of things, some probably more onerous than anything you or I have ever had to deal with, and yet they have somehow become top producers. What's your excuse? The one thing all top producers have in common is that they produce. They make it happen for themselves and in their lives today and every day. They are top producers because they decided at some point that there was no excuse for failure. They found their way to our business because it doesn't care about the color of your skin or your gender or your age; it doesn't care how many letters you have after your name or who your father was, or even if you have a father. It only cares about the numbers. And to many of us, that is beautiful. Let's face it, if people who have what we would see as disabilities can become top producers, what's your excuse?

The military uses basic training to get recruits into physical and mental shape for their upcoming assignments. We want to accomplish the same thing, to make sure you are in shape for prospecting. To prospect effectively, you really must be in the right frame of mind and have the proper outlook. Without it, you could be a disastrous failure at your job. Your job starts with prospecting. If you cannot prospect, you're dead. Anything else you may possess in the way of talent or brains or whatever is worthless, because without clients, you have nothing. If you can't get this right and do it well, then you should quit now, and I mean it. You'll be doing yourself, everyone in your family, and everyone in this business a big favor if you would just leave now. You won't survive in this business if you cannot prospect. It is the starting point and absolutely critical to growing a successful business.

## Mental Approach

Have you ever heard of Neuro Linguistic Programming (NLP)? According to Sue Knight, a leading thinker, author, consultant, and practitioner of NLP, it is the study of what works in thinking, language, and behavior. It is a way of coding and reproducing excellence that enables you to consistently achieve the results you want for yourself, your business, and your life. Knight explains that NLP can be looked at this way: "What we see and hear is what we think about. What we think about is what we feel. What we feel influences our reactions. Reactions become habits, and it is our habits that determine our destiny."

My business mentor, Frank Rimkus, used to tell me to go to the finest neighborhoods in the city and look at the homes. He wanted me to go into the homes that were for sale and imagine myself in one of them. He told me to think about how it would feel to use the pool, host a cocktail party, play tennis on my tennis court, chase my children on the front lawn, and relax in the study with a good book and a glass of fine port wine. I did this. In fact, I did it every week, and I *still* do it occasionally. Frank understood the power of visualization and knew that by visualizing myself in these homes, my actions each day would be aligned with the destiny of eventually owning that home. He also knew that I had to *truly* see myself in that house, as opposed to picturing it but not believing it could ever be true. Unless I believed that I could not only achieve it, but also could see myself in that life comfortably, it might not last even if I achieved it. I'd do things to subconsciously sabotage myself, because that's what people do when their lives are not aligned with what they believe they deserve or what they can see themselves living realistically.

Gail Davis, Ph.D., puts it this way in her book *High Performance Thinking for Business, Sports, and Life:* "Picture where you think you should be, how much money you should be making, how you should be treated, what kind of job you should have, even how you should look and act. Remember that the closer behavior and reality match your established picture, the more content you are with your life. Conversely, the further you are from the picture, the more dissatisfied and unhappy you are. Therefore, create the most accurate and detailed picture of your expectations that you can. If these pictures are positive, they are likely to reduce pressure and enhance performance . . . . Subconsciously, you will take actions that lead you to the picture, because that is what your internal picture sees as normal, comfortable, where you belong."

Nothing is more powerful than your own self-talk and visualization. For evidence of how visualization and NLP can improve performance, Gail Davis tells the story of the POW who was unable to play golf for seven years. Before becoming a POW, he shot in the 90s. In order to survive his ordeal, he visualized every stroke of every hole on his favorite course as a mental exercise. Naturally, while in isolation for five and a half years, he had physically deteriorated. Yet, the first time on the course after his release, he shot 74.

There is no way to give NLP its due here, but it is a very powerful concept. If you want to study it further, I encourage you to educate yourself by buying and reading an excellent book on the subject, *NLP at Work,* by Sue Knight (Nicholas Brealey Publishing, London). You can start to use NLP simply by putting a motivating statement somewhere where you will read it each day. Mine is on my bathroom mirror. It's been taped there for years. Although what it says is very private to me, suffice it to say, the statement acts as a trigger to psyche me up for the day. It reminds me that my performance is important and that *every* day is important. When I look at the statement each morning, I acknowledge that I have a lot of people who count on me to perform at my best every day—my family, my clients, my teammates, and my firm. What the statement says isn't important, it's whatever you need to help get you get in the frame of mind to perform at your best.

NLP is very useful in business, particularly in sales. As the name implies, it can be used as a method of increasing your performance and your life's results using language (think "self-talk") to program your actions, behaviors, and reactions. Practiced successfully, you will align your actions and behaviors in such a manner that they will lead to the results you want.

A good example of this is weight loss. A few years ago, I found myself weighing in at almost 300 pounds, totally out of shape and miserable. I asked myself one day how this could have happened to a former professional athlete? The answer was simple. My behavior and habits had resulted in my nearly 300-pound body. It was nothing other than that. It wasn't because I had a chemical imbalance. It wasn't because I had a thyroid problem. I just ate the wrong stuff at the wrong time of day and didn't exercise at all anymore! There was no one or nothing to blame except myself.

Finally, when I couldn't stand it another day, I went to an expert on weight control and nutrition. I listened to what he had to say, and started eating what he said to eat at the time of day he said to eat it. I also started to exercise a bit. I visualized myself back at my ideal weight, playing actively with my children and participating in martial arts. My eating habits, actions, and behaviors became closer in alignment with the visual picture of what I wanted to look like, and my body shape moved that direction. I dropped approximately 75 pounds and now weigh almost exactly the same as I did back when I played professional baseball.

Try this. Visualize yourself in the corner office or the location you desire at your company. You're doing exceptionally well and considered one of the top producers. Everybody respects you and you have excellent working relationships with your coworkers. You drive the car of your dreams, you live in the home you desire, and you wear the finest clothes with no regard to cost. You work the hours you enjoy working and you do the things you do best during your workday. You have great clients who think the world of you because of everything you've done for them.

See this picture in as much detail as possible. Close your eyes and see every piece of it—the items in your office, the rug on the floor, the detail of the lighting, the details of the desk and the items on it, your computer screens, everything. Visualize this every day. Take time every day to close your eyes and see the picture clearly. Become comfortable with yourself in that picture. See yourself at the desk, on the phone talking to prospects, and in important meetings with your best clients. Now, when you open your eyes, you see where you are. Not the same picture? Right. Feel uncomfortable? Yes. Why? Because you changed your frame of reference. You don't belong where you are; you belong in that picture. Soon, your actions will take you to the place where you are most comfortable in your mind. Your behavior will take you to the place where you see yourself most often in your internal mental movie. You'll start to make the outbound calls you need to make.

I know that in order for me to get to my mental picture, I need to do a certain amount per year in production and open a certain number of new, large relationships. How am I going to get there? I know what I have to do. I have to meet certain types of people and I have to meet a lot of them. I have to do it sooner rather than later. So I call and book appointments with them. Then I go see them, we talk, and I ask for their business. Only by doing this over and over will I get to my place of comfort.

How can I replace a behavior that is inhibiting my progress with one that will create my success and get me to my visualized happy place? First, identify the behavior that you want to change. Perhaps you are not making enough new business calls. You know you need to make more, but picking up the phone and doing it just doesn't seem to happen each day. Now identify the thing that is getting in your way, the specific thoughts or distractions that are causing this behavior. In many cases in our business, it is the fact that the market is open and moving. We want to watch the market, to watch CNBC or CNN. We have people coming and going in our office all the time with this and that request, the phone is ringing with clients calling for various things, and you have a ton of e-mails to catch up on or respond to. There's just so much to do that will *not* create new business, but you're still working hard, right? Right. You are working hard. You're just not doing what will take you to your happy place. You're doing what will get you farther from your happy place.

The next thing to do is rank all those things that cause the bad action to happen (or keep the good action from happening), with the highest being the one with the greatest impact on the situation. In my case, my ranking looked like this:

1. Market moving

2. E-mails

3. CNBC

4. Team members with questions and issues

5. Clients calling

Now, what action will take you to your happy place? What do you need to start doing that you're not doing now? What action needs to be taken? The answer is the action with which you want to replace the current actions. In my case, it's a list of people I need to call either to make appointments or to close deals. I get closer to my happy place if I'm asking for the order or if I'm meeting new people. Simple.

Eliminate 1, 2, and 3. Turn off the computer and the television and you've done it. Now, you have nothing to do at your desk other than the replacement action that will take you closer to your happy place.

This is one way you can use NLP techniques to create the results you desire. If you don't visualize where you want to be, your inner compass has no destination to pull you toward. Unfortunately, in business, you can't just stand still. You lose business. Someone else who *isn't* standing still will take it away from you. So, if you're not moving forward, in essence you're moving backward. The insidious thing about this is that it creeps up on you. Suddenly you wake up and you see that you're in a really bad place and wonder how you got there. Don't let that happen to you. Give yourself a destination, visualize it, and eliminate the behaviors that are preventing you from getting there. Replace them with the behaviors that *will* get you there.

## Physical Appearance

All kinds of studies have shown that the person who is six-foot tall or more, who has blond hair and looks like Jack Armstrong, will do better in sales than us average looking folks. I think those studies are full of crap. Of course, you have to look clean and neat, have a good smile, and get your haircut regularly. But in terms of the six-foot guy doing better than the five-foot guy—the athlete doing better than the nerd—in sales, I think if you don't make an offensive first impression, it's what comes after the first impression that counts. Especially if you're a man. I hate to say it, but it's true. Men are judged much more on their personalities than they are on their looks. It's unfair, but that's the way it is. It's not that men care less about the way they look, nor is it that people don't appreciate a great looking man. But in business, a man who knows his stuff, who has a pleasingly outgoing personality (as opposed to an *obnoxiously* outgoing personality), and who is not repulsive to look at, can do every bit as well as a man who looks like a model. Sometimes better. How many times have you seen a drop-dead gorgeous woman hanging on the arm of some guy who looks like your Uncle Sol?

The point is, look sharp. Be well dressed. I didn't say "wear a suit," I said "be well dressed." Don't wear cheap clothing or shoes. Get your shirts and blouses professionally pressed. Shine and take care of you shoes. Make sure your hair is cut and cared for regularly. Go to the dentist four times a year instead of two. Ladies, have your nails done often so they look sharp all the time.

## Business Approach

Just as your business should have two or three streams of revenue, your prospecting machine should have multiple streams of prospects that fit your model. This is where it can be easy to get off track. You're prospecting, and you run across prospects that appear to want to do business with you, but they don't fit your model. For one reason or another, they won't give you the ball and let you run with it. They won't even give the ball to an outside group of managers. They are control freaks. They want you to do business you don't feel good about or are outside your two or three focused lines of business. Because of the effort that goes into prospecting, you're tempted to proceed down the path with them despite these things, particularly when times are tough and *any* prospect seems hard to find.

Don't go there. But don't waste your work, either. You should know someone in the office that will take that type of account. Bring that colleague in right away and negotiate a little something for the lead. I'd say 10 to 20 percent of the first-year business with the client is fair. Your colleague will be doing all the work, and it's an account you would or should have walked away from anyhow.

As we look closer at the prospecting machine you are becoming, let's review some of the more popular ways to obtain new business.

## Advisors and Insurance Agents

These people have to have a clear understanding of what you do. You must paint a picture for them that clearly defines exactly what you're looking for in new business, so that when they see the opportunity you most desire, you are the one they think of first, not someone else. With insurance agents, you want to work with those who bring you the investment business and who are not trying to do that business themselves. These are usually very high-end insurance brokers who deal with very wealthy business owners and other affluent people. They make plenty of money handling the insurance aspects of these people's lives, and have no interest in the money management business. Ideally, you want to have a mutual understanding with the insurance guys. When they meet someone or acquire a new client who needs money management, they refer that person to you. By the same token, when you meet someone or acquire a new client who needs insurance advice, you return the favor. It's a mutual referral understanding.

## Human Resources (HR) Departments

Every major company has a need within the HR department for somewhere it can refer individuals who are retiring or leaving the firm. The people who work in the HR departments know when someone is leaving, usually before anyone else. They are an early point of entry for a professional like you. The heads of HR are concerned with making excellent recommendations. They are personality-oriented people who will try to fit the individual with someone he or she can trust and be comfortable with. The HR people may have two or three other people they will recommend in addition to you, but getting into those lists of candidates can produce a steady stream of referrals. The bigger the companies, the better, because there are more people who can use your services.

Another way to attack this is to surround the company. Once you have the HR people on board and you are someone they recommend to employees leaving the company, hopefully you can get to a point where you can call into the company directly and go after the *current* employee base. You'll want to target the 45 to 55 year olds. The more of them you can get on board, even with smaller accounts, the larger the payday will be when they start retiring and leaving. Their 401(k) plans can be very large.

I recently heard a story about a man who retired from a large company after 25 years with a 401(k) account of $4 million. He was going to convert his entire portfolio to bonds and would be making more income from his 401(k) account than he ever made working at the company. It only takes 50 people like that at one large company for you to have $200 million under management and be making $2 million or so in gross annual fees.

### Existing Clients

Let's say you have 10 ideal client relationships. You need 40 just like them to complete the business. Go to each client and tell him or her that you truly appreciate the relationship you have, and that you wish you had a few more just like it. Explain that looking for clients takes up a great deal of time, time you'd rather be spending figuring out how to help your *existing* clients save money on their taxes. Then simply ask for their help. "Who do you know that may be wealthy enough to make use of my expertise to the fullest, who would appreciate the higher level of service and attention I give my clients? What about one of your doctor friends? What about your lawyer? What about a business associate?" Prompt clients by giving them suggestions so the names of good prospects will start to pop into their heads. You'll be surprised how many referrals you may leave with.

With existing clients, or when prospecting using the model city approach, you need to pull out the magic referral technique that I introduced in my first book. You know quite a lot about your existing clients. You know their business, where they live, where they went to college, what clubs they belong to, their hobbies, where the kids go to school, and the charities they support. With that information you can compile a list of other well-to-do people they may know through one of these associations. You're looking to put together a one-page list, two columns, double spaced, with the names of 30 to 40 people that they probably know. You present the client with this list face to face. You show them that this is an internal list of individuals the firm has identified as high-priority prospective clients. The list has been screened to make sure that anyone currently doing business with the firm with another advisor is not on the list.

You tell the client that you have been assigned this list of people, and that the way it works is that you have to make every attempt to get a face-to-face meeting with them after verifying they should be on the list.

You ask for help. You've already positioned yourself with this individual as someone who handles no more than 50 relationships, so he or she knows you are very selective in whom you handle as a client. This client understands that you are looking for someone at least as wealthy as he or she is. Make sure there is a pen handy. Here's what happens most of the time: The client takes the list from you and instinctively reaches for the nearby pen. Looking over the list carefully, he or she starts to make comments as people are recognized. These comments are the key to the whole process here. Listen very carefully to what is said. Log it into your brain. Don't write anything down. Just log it into your memory bank. When the client is finished, simply say thanks, take the list back, and put it away in your briefcase. Say nothing more about it. The moment you're alone, write down everything you can about what the client said.

Later, when you have a chance to look over the list, note which names your client made a mark next to. That probably indicates recognition. You can go back to the client in a few days and ask if it would be all right if you used his or her name when you called so-and-so on the list. "Can I use your name—not as a recommendation, of course, but just as a reference point? Or, would you prefer that I just called on this person without using your name?" "Is there a way you would suggest I approach this person? What kind of guy is he? Should she be on our list?" You can generate as many as ten really nice referrals from each client this way.

## Direct Mail Campaigns

You may be easily tempted into the belief that a mail campaign of some sort is a way to drive business to you, and it may be one way to do just that, if done properly. However, considering the cost of mailing, which is continuing to increase each year, you have to recognize that the value of such campaigns can be less than satisfactory. Let me give you a real life example. A few years ago, I was with a large firm with a very well-recognized name. The firm spent millions annually to make sure it had brand identity in the market on par with no one else in the industry. We had entire departments of people who were designing direct-response mail pieces for us to send out to the world announcing various products. I decided to take advantage of all this marketing expertise and firepower and designed an excellent product to build a campaign around. I purchased lists and list management software. I had my family sitting around the house folding these pieces and stuffing thousands of envelopes every weekend and we mailed them all out. The company paid for the mailing. All it cost me was about four weekends where I subjected my children and wife to the agony of this folding, stuffing, and stacking mail campaign production line. We sent out about 5,000 pieces of mail.

Now I happen to know some pretty smart people in the mail order business. These people have informed me of the importance of list management and the complexity of direct mail list management. They agreed that it's really a neat business, but getting to be quite costly. I was informed that even the worst list with a lousy mailer should generate something around 2/10ths of 1 percent response. Well, I received one response. One. And the gentleman was eager to invest—$500. A $10 commission. Imagine my enthusiasm. My firm had spent millions on its image campaign, my manager spent a ton on the mail cost, and the firm spent a fortune designing this very professionally presented mail piece.

Here's the deal. Mailings can be successful. But doing them as a component of your prospecting is very difficult because it involves a lot of time to do the mailing and a lot of analysis to monitor the results. If changes need to be made, the cost of tracking the impact of those changes is immense—not to mention the legal maneuvering that changes require before they're made. Most of the time, in my opinion, the return on the investment doesn't justify the time and expense of mass mailings.

Granted, there are people in this business who have built entire books using this method. They will sell you a program designed to replicate their success for many thousands of dollars. I've seen people buy these and apply them and I've even seen it work for a few of them. It just doesn't work for me because I value my time very highly. Everything is a tradeoff in how you use your time. If you have some magic letter that you can mail out 1,000 and get 100 calls and land 10 decent clients, then I would call that a very successful campaign and worth every bit of effort and expense. If, however, you experience what I did, which is a huge commitment of time and money to a campaign, and the result was $10 in commissions, I think you'll agree that you could have spent that time better.

In the time it took me to do my mail campaign, I could have made 2,000 calls and reached 300 people. I probably would have booked about 30 to 50 face-to-face meetings with qualified people. Given a normal close ratio of one client for every four or five face-to-face meetings, I might have landed ten new clients. I would have spent $0 on postage, $0 on marketing material, and I would have saved about $5 on Band-Aids for my family's paper cuts.

## Invitations

The mailing of invitations, on the other hand, can work well. I've seen them used effectively by top producers at a number of firms. Although it still involves the cost of postage and the effort in the process of list acquisition and list management, if done properly, invitations can have a decidedly strong impact on your business. For example, suppose one of your target markets is the corporate executive. This individual is busy, has too much to do in his or her job and therefore doesn't often spend a lot of time analyzing his personal financial situation. You can send a personal invitation to call you at your office so that you can provide a five-minute breakdown on the potential tax implications of different types of stock options. You can enclose a return envelope and tell him or her to simply put a card in the envelope and mail it back—you'll have your assistant set an appointment for the phone call, or if he or she prefers, a face-to-face visit. The response rate may not set the world on fire, but those that do respond are very qualified in most cases and are open minded enough to listen to your ideas.

## Seminars

Seminars, if done properly, are another way to build your business. I've never done one. I'm not even qualified to tell you how to do one. I wouldn't know where to start. I do know that it involves a lot of work, just like the mailing campaign. You have to see how many are attending. You have to coordinate a location. Someone has to pay for the location. You have to make sure there are drinks and possibly food available. You have to stand up in front of a group and talk! (This may be the number one reason why most people don't do seminars.) Once you've done this, you have to follow up again and try to book appointments with the attendees in order to bring them in as clients. The bottom line for me personally is that I cannot think of anything worse than spending a half day with a bunch of people I don't know who just want to eat free food and suck investment advice and information out of me for free. Can you? Still, in all fairness, there are people who have built their entire book using this method. I'd rather call each of the people who would get the invitation in the mail and ask if I can stop by to introduce myself and show what we're doing for our best clients. Skip all the bullshit of the seminar. Let's be honest. The seminar is an educational event that is really only cloaking your real desired result, which is to get in front of people to see if you can make them your clients. You're adding a step with the seminar stuff or the mailer. If there is any truth that the people who sell more are the people who have the shorter sales cycles, then why make it longer? Why add a step to the process, not to mention the hassle and expense? Besides, the clients you want, and the clients your firm wants you to get, probably don't come to these types of things often, if ever.

## Chance Encounters

If you have a social life and are an outgoing person, inevitably you'll be running into people wherever you choose to hang out. This is why you may want to be thoughtful about where you hang out. If you hang out with a bunch of drunks in low life bars, you're not likely to meet the cream of the crop of American business society. However, if you hang out at a luxury yacht harbor, you're likely to run into some pretty cool people who have more money than exists in some small countries all piled up in one place!

## The Model City Approach

Model City is a very successful way to expand your existing business. It isn't easy, however. It takes a commitment of your time—often away from your family—and money. But it can pay off in a big way.

In Model City, you can select virtually any city in which there is a concentration of wealth that hasn't likely been tapped by someone else in your firm. Even if your company has an office in that city, if you do it correctly, you can Model City without stepping on any toes. Once you've decided where you want to go, start to gather information on the city from the chamber of commerce or the local business chronicle. Subscribe to the local paper so you can get a feel for who the players are in the town. Get the names of the people on the boards of directors of the local banks. Find out what the top country clubs are in the city and who the members are. If there is a coast or a lake, find out the name and location of the marina where the high-end boats are docked. If you can, get a list of everyone who docks there.

Once you've gathered all these names, build a database of everyone on the list and start making your Model City cold call. This is simply a slightly modified version of the regular cold call you make every day, and it goes something like this:

"Hello Mr. Johnson, this is Scott Kimball of Big Bull Securities. I don't mean to be impolite, do you have a brief minute?"

"Yes, but just one minute."

"Thanks. I'll be brief. I have been given the assignment of meeting with the right people in (Model City). We've tried to be very careful about who we're talking to because we are in the investment business, yet we don't advertise. In spite of the fact that we don't advertise, we work with some of the most affluent families in the United States, helping them manage their money wisely and providing them with a higher level of thinking when it comes to their wealth management plan. I am meeting next week with two other families that have been referred to us. Would you be kind enough to spend just a few minutes with me while I'm there?"

"Sure. When did you say you were coming here?"

"Next week. What day is good for you?"

"Wednesday is best."

"That would be fine. Can you spare the time for lunch at (Power Lunch Place) or would you prefer we just get a cup of coffee somewhere?"

"Let's just have coffee at (The Power Breakfast Place), okay?"

You now have your first meeting. One call, one conversation, one meeting. Now you do the same thing with everyone on the list. If someone can't see you this trip, but genuinely seems interested if the timing were different, make sure you note that in the database and be sure you call him or her in advance of the next trip.

You have to make about one trip every month, for at least two to four days at a time, in order to be successful using the Model City approach. Some cities take a year or even more to crack. Years ago, the senior partner on my team decided he liked Hawaii and he was going to make that his Model City. Little did we know that Hawaii is probably the toughest place to crack in the United States. It's an island, everyone fantasizes about going there and working there and writing off the trip. Every single con artist thinks he can come into the islands, rip somebody off, and disappear over the ocean and be safely out of reach.

As a result, these people are very reticent to do business with anyone they haven't known for years, particularly if you don't live on the islands. But on we charged. I was the lead cold caller and we were working out of Los Angeles. Because of the time differences, I got the luck of calling from 7 AM into Denver, then Los Angeles, then after 5 PM LA time, I shut down the LA calls and started calling Hawaii until 8 PM.

We were lucky and landed a few clients here and there, but our effort really didn't pay off for three years. To make the Model City approach work, you really need to choose a city you enjoy visiting. You had better go into it with the idea that you'll have to invest some time and money before you really see it pay off.

Using the Model City approach, the senior partner and I opened up doors and met face to face with the wealthiest people in Denver, St. Louis, Orange County, Los Angeles, and Honolulu over a five-year period. At the end of five years, we had raised in excess of $300 million for one investment product. We did this and we worked at a firm that no one had ever heard of! The firm did not advertise. We did not do seminars or mailings. We simply called people and asked them for an appointment. We had a good product and we knew how to position ourselves on the initial call to get an appointment. Once we got appointments, we knew how to obtain valuable referrals.

## Ripe Fruit Picking Is Your Business— Not Farming and Nurturing

Do you open up an account with everyone who buys a lottery ticket? After all, each and every one of them has a chance of making a fortune. No, of course you don't. Here's the point. Top Gun financial advisors work with people who have already made their money. People who have good chances of making a lot of money are not out of bounds for your book of business, but understand that most people that have money now will always have money. Most people of a certain age who do not have money now will probably end up dying that way—with no money. I know it's harsh, but that's the truth and the statistics back me up over the past 50 years in this country.

Understand that you may spend your time prospecting and dealing with many types of people out there in order to turn them into clients. The biggest problem is that many of them cannot or will not become *good* clients and won't tell you this up front. You have to be savvy enough to see this for yourself and manage your time with them. Remember, time is one of your most valuable assets—wasting it means mediocrity or failure. Here are the types of people you will run into in the prospecting effort as it relates to their wealth—or lack of it:

- People who have money and invest it.

- People who have no money but look like they have a lot of money.

- People who have high incomes but no money.

- People who have tons of money but look like paupers.

- People who have power but no money.

- People who married money.

- People who inherited money and control it.

- People who inherited money and don't control it.

- People who know people with a lot of money and have influence over them.

- People who know people with a lot of money and have no influence over them.

The Top Gun prospecting machine is a team of people led by you. Your team wants to be led, and the thing we learn from the Top Gun pilots and Navy SEAL teams is that you lead best by doing it yourself. The squad commander of a SEAL team is out in front on the training and the missions. Every member of the team should be the best or desire to be the best at his or her respective role. Each member of the team should be a student of his or her area of expertise and understand that only if the team wins, only if the mission is accomplished, does he or she win as well. Your team cannot be set up so that no matter what happens, one person is at risk and the others aren't. Everyone wins or loses, lives or dies, gets rich or doesn't, based on the success or failure of the mission. Everyone should know that there is a simple way for everyone to see whether you're pulling your weight or not, a way to identify your contribution to the team and to the mission's success, a way in which you will be judged. In this way, you create an atmosphere of responsibility, of accountability, a sense of being the best, a sort of esprit de corps. People want to work for a team like that, and more importantly, investors and others want to do business with a group of people like that.

Prospecting doesn't have to be difficult. Although I've given you a lot of information here, don't think you have to do all of it. In fact, if you only do one thing, I would suggest you make ten outbound calls to new people every day for twenty business days. If you do this, you will already be doing what 90 percent of people in our business fail to do, which will start you on the way to being a Top Gun, to being in the top 10 percent of the industry. Good luck.

# CHAPTER NINE

# REAL TOP GUN PROSPECTING STORIES

A story is often the best way to teach and the best way to learn. I asked Top Guns from all over the country to send in their real prospecting stories so we could bring them to you, and they did. In reading through them, I found that certain themes popped up frequently and that they fell into these main categories:

- Sale of business

- Relocation

- Low-tech businesses

Many of the stories were of calls in which an advisor, simply by "doing his or her pushups," making their outbound calls each day, ran across someone selling a company. These calls happened to find the person at the right time, before the sale, and allowed the advisor to get in front of the person and propose a course of action that resulted in the landing of an excellent client. Proves the saying, "The harder you work, the luckier you get," doesn't it?

Another common theme was connecting with someone who had just relocated into town. It seems that both in the company sale and the relocation situation, the importance of finding "money in motion," a phenomenon we discussed earlier in this book, proves to be a winner. People undergoing significant changes in their lives seem to be more open to hearing new ideas, and may be open to making other changes as well. They may not be interested in changing things ever again, so these moments are prime time for the advisor looking to grow his or her business.

Finally, in looking at the prospects who became great clients for these Top Guns, I observed that most were decidedly low tech. They were not trust babies who inherited millions or jet-setting rock stars, but they were ranchers and farmers, they were owners of hardware store chains, construction companies, engineering and architectural firms, sand and gravel pits, garbage collection companies, rendering plants, tire stores, and processing plants, and they were franchisees. This is where the wealth of America can be found. They live well, but modestly. They are everyday people who work hard, usually for many years, and have built something of value. They employ many people. Most importantly, they are *everywhere*. We just have to get in front of them, one on one, one by one, face to face.

## The Lawnmower Man

One day as J.T. drove through his town, he passed a house he had always admired. Huge lawns surrounded an antebellum style home with huge pillars, a true masterpiece in southern design right out of a movie set. As he slowed down to view the property, he noticed a man on a riding mower cutting the lawn. This man looked like he could be the owner of the property! Wouldn't that be a kick if it were true? Well, J.T. decided to stop his car, run across the lawn, and talk to the man on the mower. "This is insane," he said to himself while he, in his suit, ran full tilt across the vast lawn. As he approached, the man powered down the motor and looked at J.T. as if he were crazy. J.T. hollered that he had driven past the house for a few years and had always admired it and wondered who lived there. "So today, when I saw you, I decided to come and talk. Are you the owner?" The man was as gracious as the home behind him, and he said that indeed he was.

J.T., by taking this bold action, began a dialogue with someone he might have normally never had a chance of meeting. He eventually landed an account by bringing the trust and estate people of his firm into the loop.

## The Cake Lady

Bill lived in a city that was experiencing growth. Suburbs were growing quickly in all directions, with new homes being built at a rapid pace. Bill liked to drive around new subdivisions on the weekend and look at the new homes. But he had a motive other than simply seeing new houses—he used this method to prospect.

On one Saturday, Bill saw a huge moving van unloading into a very nice new home. He stopped and asked one of the moving men if the owner was around. She was and Bill introduced himself. He welcomed her to town and asked where she came from. She replied that she had moved from Chicago and offered Bill some cake and a cool drink. After about a 20-minute conversation, Bill left with a check for an initial $50,000 to open an account. The owner later had her old account transferred to Bill from Chicago, and it became a seven-figure account, as this lady had been the beneficiary of life insurance from her husband and had relocated to be closer to her children and grandchildren.

## The Truck King

Using the Standard & Poors Directory of Companies and Executives, Jerry called a company named Truck Center. He asked for the owner by name as listed in the directory, and was frankly surprised that the owner jumped on the line almost immediately. Jerry was at the time a 22-year-old caller for a 40-year-old advisor. He explained that they were offering a special deal only to qualified clients, those people with over $1 million in liquid assets. The owner, Harold, said he qualified. Jerry booked the appointment for his advisor to see Harold. The advisor, on hearing how easy the appointment was set up, had Jerry call back and make sure the guy was qualified. Jerry explained that they were looking forward to meeting, but that he wanted Harold to know that this deal was for truly qualified people. Harold, always the gentleman, simply said, "I heard you the first time you said it, son. If your boss there doesn't believe I'm qualified, let him know that I make around $3 million per year and have for the past ten years."

Jerry's advisor took him along to the meeting. They sat down in the man's office, which was located in the middle of an enormous paved parking lot filled with huge trucks. As the advisor explained the deal, Harold stayed quiet and listened, nodding occasionally. When the advisor stopped talking, Harold said thanks, stood up, and extended his hand. When asked if he had any questions, Harold said no, but that he would call at the end of the week with an answer.

When Harold called Jerry, he said, "Jerry, I'll do a million of the deal. And let me know when you have any more things like this." That was it. Jerry went down and signed him up. He participated in virtually every offering of that type for years and became a huge client for Jerry and his advisor.

## The Junk-Food King

Larry was calling on business owners in Orange County to pitch a money management system sponsored by his firm that had a $1 million minimum. One company owner, named Jim, told Larry that normally he wouldn't have any interest. He'd basically invested in his company for many years, but a larger company recently had offered to buy his company, and he was probably going to accept the offer within a month or so. He told Larry to come on over the next day and show the product to him.

The next day, Larry showed up at a building in an industrial part of town. The air had a pungent odor, and the building had offices in front and a large enclosed section with no windows behind it. The total size appeared to be around 100,000 square feet, but Larry couldn't see what was beyond the front office area. The parking lot was full. Larry was showed into Jim's office where Jim sat casually dressed. Nothing in the surroundings gave Larry a clue what Jim's company did. So he asked, "Jim? What do you guys do around here?"

Jim smiled and said, "I put the *junk* in junk food." Larry obviously looked puzzled, so Jim jumped up and said, "Come on. I'll show you." The rear of the building was huge and open, filled with large machines and conveyer belts. Jim explained that his machines took potato chips that had no flavoring, sprayed them with a thin coat of oil, and then dusted them with the powdered flavoring. He was a subcontractor of one of the large chip companies for their West Coast distribution.

## The Garbage Man

Roger was given a number of dormant accounts by the branch manager one day. He welcomed the stack of cold clients, as he hadn't had any luck cold calling lately. On about the third call, he spoke with Conrad, the name of the person on the account. Conrad said that he thought the account had been closed. Roger explained that it had been dormant, but that there was still $40 in the account, probably interest that had hit the account after he withdrew most of his money. Roger then asked if there was anything going on that Conrad wanted to talk about. What a great question! Conrad told Roger that he had just that week received $1.8 million in cash and another smaller sum in stock for his garbage disposal business.

Roger immediately asked where the money had been deposited. Conrad said that it was in a Treasury bill at the local bank. Roger then told Conrad that he was coming up to see him. Even though Conrad objected, Roger was firm. Roger suggested that the funds were in a T-bill only because Conrad didn't know what else to do with them, and pointed out that his job was to help people figure out how to invest money like that in a way that would keep it safe but earn them a decent return, certainly more than a 6-month Treasury bill.

That afternoon, Roger went up and found the company. The owner had a small box of an office above the equipment and sorting operations below. Conrad sat there at a junky desk filled with papers. The office apparently hadn't been cleaned since the company was started. Dust was everywhere. A dog on the floor didn't move.

Conrad made Roger wait around for an hour while he talked on the phone, then they talked for about 40 minutes. Roger learned that there were two other partners in the business. Roger decided that the best way to handle this was to have all three of them into the office to open accounts as soon as possible. All three were to bring in the stock and discuss investing the proceeds of a stock sale and any cash they had received. Roger insisted, however, that Conrad immediately transfer the Treasury bill into an account at Roger's firm. Conrad agreed.

A few days later, all three garbage men showed up in the office in their jeans and work boots. They squeezed into Roger's small office and they joked around. Roger made them feel at ease, made them feel good about working with him. At the end of the meeting, all three had opened accounts and deposited their stock and cash, and they agreed to talk individually about their future plans. After Roger befriended one of them in particular, the former garbage man led Roger into meetings with several regional waste disposal companies that were being sold to public companies. Roger began subscribing to *Waste News*, the industry publication, and found many leads there.

## The Franchisee

Everyone knows that a successful franchise business can be lucrative, but when you have not one, but 100 locations, you can have a real business. That's what happened to Frank when he called on a nondescript business in the city in which he lived and worked. The company was listed as a management company in the directory and Frank thought that perhaps they managed real estate, such as apartment buildings, or some such.

It turned out that they managed a number of fast food restaurants—100 locations to be exact, and had annual revenues of approximately $100 million. And there was one owner—100 percent held by one man.

This man had a problem. He made so much money that he didn't know what to do with it. He had invested it—he lived modestly. His biggest concern was that he was paying exorbitant tax bills. He didn't mind paying some taxes, but this was ridiculous! All the net income of the business came through on his personal tax return!

Frank's angle was to get in front of the franchisee and, instead of talking about investing his money, to deal with his pain. He let the man get out on the table how much this problem bothered him, and how much it bothered him that his advisors couldn't find a decent solution to the problem. Frank told him that he wouldn't talk about investments, but rather, he would come back in a week with the right person to solve this problem. If that worked out, he asked, would it be all right if he moved at least half his investment business to Frank? The man agreed, but he said that he didn't think Frank could do it. Frank said that he would be there exactly one week later, to put it in his appointment book.

Frank hired his college friend and tax attorney to help him sit in on the meetings he had in mind. He then went to the top partners at the best CPA firms in the country, explaining that he was doing a search for a very wealthy client with a tax problem, and asked them to bring a well-thought-out solution to the specific problem. He scheduled back-to-back meetings in his office and interviewed ten groups. He invited three back the next day for longer sessions and made a selection. The selected team understood that they did not have the business yet, that only the owner of the business could make that final call, but that in Frank's opinion, they were the best group with the best plan of action and solution for the client.

One week later Frank arrived at the office with the tax people. He introduced them, explained the selection process, and let the tax people present their thinking.

Needless to say, this became a massive account for Frank and for the firm. The fee business was over $2 million per year for this one relationship. Sometimes, you have to do the extraordinary to win the extraordinary client. It doesn't always work out. Sometimes you do the extraordinary and the client doesn't appreciate it or you can't find the solution. But often it does work out, and the result can be that you land a client that changes your life forever.

## The Advisor to the Stars

Harry liked to access clients through their tax advisors. He had always been good at working with tax advisors or CPAs, because Harry had been an accountant himself some years before. Instead of cold calling potential clients, Harry cold called CPAs, took them to lunch, and networked with them. Harry naturally knew what CPAs liked and feared in a financial person, and he worked hard to show them that he was someone they could trust with their best clients.

Ron, a CPA in Los Angeles, agreed to meet with Harry because he had just inherited a practice from a partner who had suddenly retired. Ron needed help with some of these clients, and quickly, because some of them were very wealthy and relied on him not just for accounting and tax work, but more as a business manager. Ron was, after all, located in Beverly Hills, and his clients were some of the most famous and successful writers and producers in town. Harry didn't know any of this when he called—Ron had just said, "Sure, I'll meet you. Get over here."

As it turned out, Harry was in the right place at the right time. Ron needed someone to execute transactions and place assets, to make asset allocation suggestions and decisions, and to analyze portfolios for him while he worked on all the other business matters for his clients, which were many. Harry virtually became an employee of Ron's for the next six months, working out of both his own and Ron's office as he shuttled information back and forth. He opened accounts for Ron's clients, and started the process of taking each portfolio apart and putting it back together again, developing a plan for each, making Ron look like a hero to his new-found clients.

This one relationship produced over $400,000 in annual revenue for Harry every year, and after the first year, in which Harry worked very hard, the amount of time involved was minimal.

## The New CEO

For a full year, Greg had been calling the senior executives at this one computer company in a town about a five-hour drive away. He had crossed off those that had told him no, but there were a few that hadn't yet, so he kept on calling. One day, he noticed that one of the senior vice presidents, Ken, who had told him no and said not to bother him as he was retiring, had just been named CEO of a company literally down the street from Greg's office. Greg immediately picked up the phone and called him at the new company. When he talked to the assistant, he gave his name and said that Ken would remember him because he had called Ken 100 times over the past year, and that he wanted to welcome him to town.

This approach worked. As Ken had been fairly aloof and distant in the past, his change in position to CEO of an exciting, young, growing company on the edge of technology advancement and his move to a new city, all added up to make Ken an entirely different person as he got on the phone with Greg and invited him to come on over. It was a reward for a year's worth of work. Ken became a top client and eventually sold the firm to a Fortune 100 company. Greg actually went on to become a personal financial consultant to Ken and helped him over the next few years to build a company in the leisure business.

## The Treasurer

Mike read that a company in town had sold one of its divisions to an Israeli-based company. It didn't seem like a big deal, no terms were disclosed, but Mike called the treasurer. He asked Tom, the treasurer, "Did you take cash or stock for the sale?" Tom said that it was both. As it turned out, the cash was $100 million and the stock was worth about $85 million. The problem with the stock was that it didn't trade in the United States and was a fairly illiquid stock on the two exchanges that it did trade on.

Mike immediately made a case for placing the certificate with his firm. He had trading desks in London and Germany and could trade the stock on both desks. He would personally get up in the middle of the night and be in for trading in London, and work the trade with the traders in London from his desk in the United States. He got the stock. He then made a case for moving in the cash. He showed how the cash would be managed according to the company's investment policy statement, and showed Tom how the cash would achieve a better after-tax rate of return if managed a certain way. He won the cash business.

Over the next six months, the stock was sold. Mike was in every night at 2:00 AM handling the trades until 9:00 AM when London closed, then working on U.S. business until around 2:00 PM, when he went home and went to bed. He did this every day until all the stock was sold. He then handled the conversion from pounds to dollars and delivered the cash into the cash management account that his firm ran on a fee basis. In total, this relationship paid Mike over $400,000 in two years. According to Mike, it was not only profitable business, but fun as well.

## The Orthos

Jason was cold calling at 5:30 on a Friday night when he actually got an orthodontist on the telephone. The doctor told Jason that his timing was excellent because he had participated in a private investment in an orthodontic company some time ago, and that company was looking to go public very soon. The doctor provided the appropriate contact names at the company when Jason asked.

Over the course of the next few months, Jason was able to bring his services to the company and convince them to allow him to handle all the stock business for the insiders and the shareholders that were scattered throughout the country. In the next few months, Jason brought in over $300 million in assets and produced over $800,000 from this one relationship alone. And all this started as a cold call on a Friday at 5:30 PM, long after most people in this business have gone home.

I hope the lessons in this book and the stories of actual prospecting successes have given you the encouragement to keep going, to keep doing your pushups, particularly when the markets get tough. Having a job on Wall Street is an honor. Most of the people who come to this industry cannot stay here. It is too fast, too tough, too demanding. Like in battle, your success or failure is felt quickly and is not something that can be hidden, in most cases. This business is the closest thing to war or competitive sports that I know of. That's what makes it exhilarating, but also what makes it a business of warriors.

Your relentless pursuit of excellence; your ability to take more rejection than the next guy; your ability to move faster, be smarter, act bold in the face of fearsome market conditions; your ability to lead others when the going gets tough; these are the traits that will make you successful. Good luck to you. If you there is anything you don't understand about this book, or if you just have a question or story you wish to share, do something about it. Use this e-mail address: dskimball1@aol.com.

D. Scott Kimball is a managing director for one of Wall Street's largest investment banks. He has spent twenty years on Wall Street, starting at E.F. Hutton while studying economics and political science at UCLA. He is the creator of a successful NYSE listed derivative, been involved in mergers and acquisitions, and currently manages long/short equity investments for private clients.

He is a member of the Association for Financial Professionals, the National Association for Business Economics, the American Economics Association, the National Association of Investment Professionals, and the Association for Investment Management Sales Executives. Prior to entering Wall Street, he was a professional baseball player with the Toronto Blue Jays Baseball Organization. He now resides in Atlanta, Georgia, with his family.